Adventures of a Ballet Historian

Adventures of a Ballet Historian

AN UNFINISHED MEMOIR

by Ivor Guest

FOREWORD BY MARY CLARKE

WITH A BIBLIOGRAPHY COMPILED BY

SELMA LANDEN ODOM

Dance Books Ltd., London

ISBN 0-903102-69-2

Dance Books Ltd., 9 Cecil Court, London WC2N 4EZ, England

Frontispiece: Ivor Guest, photo by Jennie Walton.

Jacket and interior design by Bert Waggott

Contents

List of Illustrations

ℱoreword

WHEN Ivor Guest asked me to write the foreword to his book of memoirs—happily subtitled "Unfinished"—he said it was because I had known him longer than anyone else in ballet. Not quite true, perhaps, for when we first met he already knew Richard Buckle who was publishing his first articles in *Ballet*. But true in the sense that for over thirty years we have been close colleagues, working in different areas of ballet—my concern has been mostly with the present, his with the past—but sharing many enthusiasms and enjoying together many performances.

I knew Ivor before his first book (the one on Napoleon III) was published, at the time when he was collating all the material and the illustrations for his *Ballet of the Second Empire*. I was living in Dulwich at the time and on many Sundays would take the train four stations down the line to spend the day at his parents' house and mull over with him the new discoveries he had made. I remember my excitement when he showed me the pictures he had found in what we used to call "the black boxes" at the Paris Opéra and I remember how warm was his passion for the dancers of the Romantic period when he moved backwards in time to that golden age. (I also remember his mother saying wistfully that she wished he would fall in love with someone who had not been dead for nearly one hundred years.)

Reading these memoirs brings back for me a host of recollections but also fills in lots of gaps. Usually he would tell me when he had made an important find and often describe how, sometimes by coincidence at the end of much patient research, he had established a vital date. But he was too modest to reveal quite how much time and devotion went into his work.

The story, now I come to read it in full, is a marvelous one. Ivor, by charting his experience, has shown the way for future historians and has provided them with a body of works of inestimable value. The accuracy of his work and the amount of factual information so lovingly given in all the appendices place every writer on dance for ever in his debt. I think the story will be interesting to anyone who cares about ballet's history; to those of us who know and treasure Ivor's books it will be very precious.

The subtitle as I have said is "An Unfinished Memoir"; it could equally have been subtitled "The Memoirs of a Happy Man." As Ivor explains, things worked out wonderfully for him. During the years of basic researching, when every holiday was spent in the Museum of the Paris Opéra, he was living with his parents and could thus combine the twin careers of his law practice and his ballet writing with no domestic responsibilities. Having established himself securely in both fields, he did fall in love with someone very much alive and in Ann Hutchinson found the ideal partner. To a happy career was added a happy marriage. I think I'm doubly qualified to write this—I knew Ann before Ivor did.

MARY CLARKE

Adventures of a Ballet Historian

CHAPTER ONE

Seeds of an Obsession

DANCING played a negligible part in my upbringing. As a boy I was gifted with a natural aptitude for sport, and although inclined to be physically lazy, I ended my schooldays at Lancing as the winner of the Open High Jump and the opening fast bowler in the cricket team. If anyone in those days had suggested I should study dancing, I would have scornfully refused, and in fact I have never really mastered the simplest ballroom dances, although my wife, who should know, tells me I am promising material if only I would persevere! I have to admit that dancing was an activity that was both foreign and inimical to me. Being shy by nature, I never enjoyed going to dances, and when I did go, the greatest pleasure came when I struggled out of my stiff shirt at the end of the evening—the same sort of physical relief I felt at the end of a dress parade of the Officers Training Corps, when I exchanged the prickly khaki uniform and tight puttees for comfortable gray flannel trousers.

The theatre and the cinema exerted a powerful fascination over me from an early age—it was my childhood ambition to become a Hollywood film director—but I can recall no emerging interest in the dance. I did not see Pavlova, nor the Ballet Russe companies

that were appearing in London when I was in my teens. My introduction to ballet took place about 1937, when a great-aunt took me
to Sadler's Wells to see the Vic-Wells Ballet, but my memories of
that evening are vague. I recall that I saw Fonteyn and Helpmann in
Apparitions, but I am ashamed to confess that they produced no
overwhelming revelation.

It was at this time that I was discovering the joys of writing.
During my holidays from school my brother and I would prepare
plays which we presented on a toy stage before small audiences of
indulgent relatives and friends. These productions became more and
more ambitious, progressing from the Victorian melodrama *The
Miller and his Men,* for which we used the "penny-plain tuppence-
colored" sheets, to grand historical spectacles which I wrote and
designed myself. One of these was *Jane the Quene* (sic), a tear-
jerker about Lady Jane Grey, partly plagiarized from Harrison
Ainsworth, which closed with a scaffold scene that made a dear old
friend of the family weep real tears, and another, *The Course of
Destiny,* a drama based on the friendship of Napoleon III and Louise
de Mercy-Argenteau. Among my juvenilia were other plays and
short stories which gave me much pleasure to write but have long
since been consigned to the flames.

My imagination had been strangely stirred by the poignant imper-
manence of human life that the study of history revealed to me. I
believe I have always had an instinctive insight into other periods of
time—a gift which in my early years, before I understood it, produced moments of terror. As a very young child I had a horror of
fancy dress parties, and while strange masks may scare any child, I
see now that in my case it was because the costumes were stirring
strong emotions I could not comprehend. One of the few violent
scenes I have made was when my mother thought to send me to a
party wearing a boy's suit from the Regency period that had been
handed down in the family. The very feel of the cloth was repug-
nant; it was as though I were being wrapped in a shroud. Happily,
this aversion seems to have had no serious effect on my personality,
and I eventually went willingly to fancy dress parties so long as I
was disguised as a Red Indian.

Until I was about fifteen, history as a school subject repelled me,
but then, thanks to the inspiration given me by my history master at
Lancing, Christopher ("Monkey") Chamberlain, my imagination
was suddenly fired. In my last two years at school I read widely
and—like many another boy—found myself carried away by the romantic rise and fall of Napoleon. Then this not uncommon hero-

worship took another turn. Through the vivid writing style of Philip Guedalla I discovered the Second Empire and became much more fascinated by the amiable and enigmatic figure of Napoleon III. The fact that the house in Chislehurst in which I was born overlooked the little Catholic church where that unfortunate Emperor was laid to rest may have helped to stimulate this interest, which gripped me more and more with each book I read.

My thirst for knowledge about the Second Empire was insatiable. Even the most trivial detail was precious in filling in the picture of the period that was building up in my mind. Expeditions to the bookshops of Charing Cross Road, and later the ferreting of my friend Harold Mortlake, produced the nucleus of a library on almost every conceivable aspect of that time. To my great delight I discovered the music of Offenbach, although at that time very little of it was recorded. And when I visited Paris for the first time in 1939, that city seemed already familiar to me from the old guidebooks of seventy or eighty years before . . . and I found myself regretting the absence of crinolines and horse-drawn omnibuses!

I was nineteen when World War Two broke out, and in 1940 I was called up into the army. I was not made for military life, which I found almost unbearably tedious, and never more so than in 1941, when I was stationed with an artillery regiment in Northern Ireland. I have never taken kindly to discomfort, and the exercises that took us from our camp for several days on end and involved sleeping in rough barns and fields were particularly unwelcome. But one of them brought me an experience that seems now, in retrospect, to have been a sort of premonition. This particular exercise had ended a day earlier than planned, and since we were many miles from our camp, we were rewarded with an undisturbed night, free from guard duties and early reveille. Falling asleep beneath a starry summer sky, I dreamed one of those vivid dreams whose magic lingers in the mind during the waking day that follows. Banal though it seems in description, I awoke with the vision of a ballerina dancing alone on a stage and a perception of sheer beauty that haunted me for many days afterwards.

Nearly a year later, when I was attending an army course in Brighton, I went to the Theatre Royal to see the Anglo-Polish Ballet. I had not been drawn there by the memory of my dream—its significance, if significance there was, did not strike me until afterwards—but was merely following a pattern of going regularly to the theatre, whatever the program. Although the standard of the company, as I came to recognize, was only second-rate, I was overwhelmed. Never had I experienced such a revelationary shock. I went back the following evening, and a few weeks later, having moved to London, I discovered the Sadler's Wells Ballet at the New Theatre. I joined the enthusiasts who hired folding stools to queue for the gallery and thus became a balletomane, worshipping at the shrines of Margot Fonteyn and Beryl Grey.

Hungrily I devoured every book on the ballet that I could lay hands on, and at home, during my leaves, I searched through my books on the Second Empire to discover what place ballet held in those days. In this way I learned of the brilliant career of Emma Livry, so tragically cut short when she was burned on the stage of the Paris Opéra, and of the last ballet to be created there before the outbreak of war in 1870—*Coppélia,* whose music wove itself into the thread of my Second Empire obsession. To me these were stirring discoveries, and surprised that such an interesting period in the development of ballet had not found its historian, I began to accumulate notes with the growing purpose of writing a book myself when better times came.

In the course of my reading I chanced upon an article in the *Dancing Times,* "The First Swanilda" by Lillian Moore, a moving account of Giuseppina Bozzacchi, the young ballerina who created the leading role in *Coppélia* and died six months later during the Siege of Paris. Sensing that the author was a researcher after my own heart, I wrote to her. When her answer reached me many months later, I had almost forgotten I had written, for my letter had followed her from New York to Hawaii, where she was dancing for U.S. servicemen. To my dismay I seem to have lost her first letter, which was to be the starting point of a correspondence and a friendship that lasted until her death in 1967.

Lillian was the first person I met who shared my passion for dance history, and for me our relationship was specially significant because it revealed the pleasures that were to be gained from sharing the excitements and discoveries of the research chase. Also, her writing had a vitality that showed me we were both striving after the same end, to bring to life through words the history and romance of ballets past in accurate and balanced detail. But there was one important difference between us—while I was a historian who had chanced upon the dance, she was a dancer who had discovered history. At the time of our first exchange of letters she already had had considerable stage experience with companies such as the American Ballet, the ballet of the Metropolitan Opera and the Fokine Ballet, and between rehearsals and performances she had burrowed most profitably in libraries and archives, assembled a fine collection of ballet prints, and turned out a stream of articles and a very reliable and readable book on the great figures in ballet history, *Artists of the Dance.* She was so inherently modest that it took time for me to appreciate the full extent of this achievement, but I knew from the beginning I had found a kindred soul.

Meanwhile, the War was running its course, and I found myself in Europe taking part, modestly, in the advance through France, Belgium and Holland into Germany. Victory came, and during the year that I still had to serve before being demobilized, I spent a number of short leaves in Brussels, one of which stands out in my memory as a special landmark. It was midwinter, and the train that carried me from the heart of Germany to the Belgian capital was unheated. Lying awake shivering, I fell to wondering what to do with my time and was struck, quite suddenly, with the thought that in the city's main library there must surely be newspapers of the Second Empire that would contain descriptions of the ballets at the Paris Opéra. So, in a state of elation, I made my way to the Royal Library, and in my own eccentric way spent several happy days working through bound volumes of *Le Figaro,* piecing together from reviews and news items the fortunes of the ballet of those distant years. I am obviously a dramatist *manqué,* for it was the tragedy in the stories of those two ill-fated ballerinas, Emma Livry and Giuseppina Bozzacchi, that provided the impetus to launch me on the study of ballet history that was to become my life's work.

The call of Paris was now irresistible. My love affair with that city had begun with the happy week I had spent there with my mother shortly before the outbreak of war in 1939. After the Fall of France a year later I became afflicted with a sentimental yearning for Paris that was uncommon in austere and beleaguered Britain, being expressed in the popular song, "The Last Time I Saw Paris." In the advance through France in 1944 I crossed the Seine some fifty miles downstream from Paris, but while I was denied the immediate joy of revisiting the city of my dreams, it had at least ceased to be inaccessible. It was possible to take my last leave in Paris, and through one of the interallied organizations I was offered hospitality by a radiologist in the Rue d'Amsterdam.

Dr. Charles Chuche was one of those larger-than-life characters— a rotund, jovial, anglophile Frenchman who prided himself on his command of idiomatic English, which was spiced by his daily reading of the Courts Day by Day column in one of the London newspapers. However, he did not always catch the nuances of cockney slang, and once referred to his wife as "my feefty-feefty," which I guessed was a corruption of the term, "my better half." I became very fond of Dr. Chuche, who understood the unusual quest that had brought me to Paris. He was also cultured and conversant with the arts, and told me that one of his clients was the ballerina Lycette Darsonval, whom I was to know in later years.

The aim I had set myself on this pilgrimage was to unearth as much information as possible about the creation of *Coppélia*. I had prepared the ground in advance by writing to the libraries that were likely to have material that would interest me. André Ménetrat, the Librarian of the Opéra, wrote me a welcoming and helpful letter, and put me in touch with Carlotta Zambelli, who answered no less warmly and in English.

Paris in 1946 was recovering from the trauma of the German Occupation, and its inhabitants were still suffering severe privations. Food—in what was traditionally a gastronome's paradise—was in such short supply that I had to collect rations from the U.S. Army PX to supplement my host's larder. Electricity was cut off completely during certain hours of the day, and paper was so short that the programs at the Opéra measured about three inches square. But people were conditioned to shortages in those days, and my rapture at finding myself in the city of my dreams was in no way dimmed by these abnormal conditions. I knew exactly what I wanted to do, and on my very first morning I set out on what I saw even then as a historic pilgrimage, bound for the Library of the Opéra. Entering this historian's Holy of Holies, I was greeted by Marcelle Morillon, one of the assistant librarians, a dear, motherly lady, now retired, who has often reminded me of my first appearance, in army uniform.

I fell immediately under the spell of the magnificent circular reading room that had originally been intended as the retiring room for the Emperor Napoleon III. No wonder that the place became my spiritual home! In the thirty years and more that have passed since my initiation, its cornucopia of treasures has shown no sign of running out, and as will later appear, exciting discoveries have continued to come my way from its vast accumulation of material. During that very first visit in 1946 I was concentrating on the original production of *Coppélia* and the life of Mlle. Bozzacchi, the original Swanilda, but I could not forget Emma Livry, and M. Ménetrat brought out for my inspection the small wooden casket containing the pathetic remnants of the charred costume she had been wearing on the evening of her terrible accident on the stage of the former opera house in the Rue Le Peletier in 1862.

It is part of the magic of the Library of the Opéra that it has none of the impersonal atmosphere usually associated with a public institution. It had, and still has, the engaging informality of a club. There is time for quiet talks, friendships are formed, sometimes a distinguished singer or dancer will come in to consult a score or a book, and however humble one may be, one's wants are always willingly attended to. Sometimes, if one is privileged, one may be invited to return after closing time to attend one of the receptions that are held there. It was on occasions of this sort that, some years later, I was to meet Serge Lifar, who had returned to his post of *maître de ballet,* and to see some ancient figures who had survived from the *belle époque,* that golden age of elegance before the first World War—Cléo de Mérode, Cécile Sorel and one of the greatest of the Opéra's Directors, Jacques Rouché. Presiding over this haven was the Pickwickian figure of André Ménetrat, the Librarian, a rather formal man who became a friend, and under him there served, in those days, three charming lady librarians, Mme. Morillon, Mme. Carol-Bérard and Mlle. Boschot.

It was not easy to tear myself away from such surroundings, but I braved the bitter January weather to carry out research in the Cabinet des Estampes of the Bibliothèque Nationale, which was temporarily housed in a mansion near the Etoile; the Bibliothèque de l'Arsenal and the Archives Nationales. Particularly evocative were the discoveries I made in the Archives, as I worked my way through the crimson boxes containing the records of the Opéra, in which even the most insignificant papers were preserved because happily it had been no one's duty to weed them out. I remember once being tempted to slip into my pocket an unused admission ticket headed "Théâtre Impérial de l'Opéra" that was serving as a marker! But more important were the first of Saint-Léon's many letters that I was to turn up over the years, giving a wonderfully vivid insight into the ballet of the 1860s, and a letter in the careful, childish handwriting of Giuseppina Bozzacchi.

Another link with Bozzacchi had been provided by Lillian Moore, who had sent me a copy of a letter she had received before the War from a Monsieur Bozzacchi, who was a nephew of the dancer. The telephone directory revealed that he was still living at the address Lillian had given me, and I paid him a call. I met him only that once, for he left his apartment in the Rue de Turenne shortly afterwards and I lost touch with him. But I can visualize him still, a quiet little man in a white coat who came into the room from, I imagined, the workbench where he exercised his jeweler's craft, to tell me what he knew about his aunt. Although it was not very much, since his father was still a baby when Giuseppina had danced in *Coppélia,* I found it very moving to meet someone of her own flesh and blood and to be shown the few modest relics the family possessed—an oil portrait of her, copied from one of Reutlinger's photographs, and a strangely heavy ring of some base metal which Saint-Léon had given her. I often wonder what became of that ring.

So limited was my knowledge of ballet history at that time that the name Carlotta Zambelli meant nothing to me until M. Ménetrat wrote to me. I soon discovered she was part of the tradition of the Opéra, having made her début there as a young ballerina more than fifty years before. When I arrived to keep our appointment at the stage door of the Opéra, she was already waiting for me, looking somewhat younger than I had expected and dressed in a sensible but unfashionable style. She led me into a world of enchantment as we made our way along corridors and up staircases that seemed to have come to life from old lithographs, and into the dressing-room that was still hers. There, on a dying January afternoon, she answered my questions about *Coppélia* in the strong Milanese accent she never lost, and showed me the signed lithograph of Carlotta Grisi that hung on the wall, its glass broken and the print itself browning from contact with the atmosphere. But what I remember most of all from that first meeting was her warmth and understanding. She put me at my ease at once, encouraging my interest in the traditions of French ballet as no one had done before. Her friendship, which I was to enjoy for twenty years, was a privilege she granted to few writers on the dance. It was also an inspiration of a very special nature, for to me she represented a living link with the past that my imagination was striving to re-create.

CHAPTER TWO

I Become a Historian

IN July 1946 I exchanged my army uniform for an equally drab pin-striped "demob" suit and joyfully became a civilian once again. The pattern of what was to become a double life was already set. Ever since my Cambridge days the law had been my chosen career, and I now had to serve for two years as an articled clerk and pass my final examination before qualifying as a solicitor. I was, as I fully appreciated, fortunate in being able to live in an atmosphere of comfort, free from financial cares, in my parents' home, and in having an opening waiting for me in the family firm.

This firm, one of the oldest in the country, can trace its history well beyond the earliest Law List. The family connection goes back to my great-great-great-grandfather, Richard Walter Forbes, who began to practice in 1787, and the firm has occupied its present London office in Lincoln's Inn Fields since 1864. In old-fashioned parlance we are basically "family solicitors" and have been lawyers, men of business and friends of numerous families for generations. In course of time I was to succeed my father and other older partners as adviser to many of these established clients, and as the firm has developed, my area of specialization has focused on trust law and the formation and administration of charities. Today, as senior partner, I work in a room which over the past 118 years has been occupied, in unbroken succession, by my great-grandfather (whose name is still painted on the door), my grandfather, my father and myself.

My career as a lawyer lies outside the scope of these reminiscences, but it has not been wholly irrelevant to my interest in the dance. People who know me only by my writing are often astonished when they discover that I am also a busy full-time lawyer. To their inevitable question, "How on earth do you manage it?" I can only reply that I suppose it is because I am well organized, have a facility for concentration and enjoy good health. I have allowed few other calls on my leisure time. While not by any means unsociable, I do not hanker after company and am never bored when alone. For many years the lure of foreign travel was satisfied by my research expeditions to Paris, and I have indulged in no sporting activities since leaving school, although my interest in cricket leads me, perhaps once a year, to Lord's to watch a day's play in the warm summer sunshine. By organizing my time I have been able to set aside out of early mornings, evenings and weekends a respectable and regular allotment of time for writing.

My legal training has not been without influence on my literary activities. In coping with a complex legal problem it is necessary to assimilate a welter of facts, arrange them in a methodical order, and then examine them, not from a single point of view (the lawyer who can only see a problem through his client's eyes certainly cannot offer the most helpful advice) but with as unbiased a detachment as one can humanly muster. In much the same way a mass of research material must be sorted out and presented. Another point of contact between the lawyer and the historian has been a sympathy for people, whose problems have to be understood by the former, and whose actions and behavior are raw material for the latter.

I am, I know, exceptionally fortunate in being able to derive great satisfaction from both my profession and my avocation. My legal interests have taken me into areas few lawyers enter, largely through my task of administering the Radcliffe Trust, the oldest of the large grant-making foundations in the United Kingdom, which supports such varied fields as astronomy, chamber music and the crafts. They have also resulted in my becoming a trustee of a number of interesting charities, including the Calvert Trust (which gives the disabled the opportunity of enjoying the Lake District) and the Dutch Church in London.

I have always preferred to keep my profession and my avocation distinct, and only once have I been involved as a lawyer in a theatrical enterprise. The experience of forming a charitable company to receive an Arts Council grant for a new ballet company, London Dance Theatre, fell within the area of my specialization, but the hassles with the theatre management and the financial backer were another matter and proved very time-consuming and exhausting. The company's London season was a commercial disaster in spite of good reviews, and the project collapsed. At my office I returned to more familiar work, but my involvement in this enterprise stirred the memory of one of the firm's old managing clerks, a man in his eighties who had been with us for over fifty years. He came into my room one day to tell me that as a boy he had worked for a firm of solicitors in the West End among whose clients had been Katti Lanner, the ballet mistress of the Empire Theatre, and he had remembered an incident when she had arrived to sign her will, and he had been called upon to be one of the witnesses. As he was leaving the room after the will had been signed, he overheard Mme. Lanner ask the solicitor whether a half sovereign would be an acceptable tip for the boy and saw her hand over the small gold coin. Some minutes later the boy was summoned again to hold open the door of Mme. Lanner's carriage as she entered it to return home, and as she drove off, the solicitor turned to the boy with the words, "Mme. Lanner very generously left me with a tip for you," and handed him a sixpence!

When I began my legal studies at Cambridge in 1938 I had no inkling of the fascinating insights into other fields of activity that my legal practice was to bring me, and I accepted the law as it was then taught to me—Roman law, the history of the English legal system, jurisprudence, the law of property, contract, tort, each filling a separate pigeonhole in my mind—as an academic process that seemed merely an extension of my school studies. It never troubled me, however, that I knew I would never fit into the conventional mold of lawyers, for I had already discovered my avocation as an historian which I was to follow no more nor less seriously than my profession.

During my years at Cambridge, history, particularly that of Second Empire France, had become such an obsession that my tutor made a vain attempt to quench it. It happened that one of the Fellows of my college, Trinity, was the Rev. F. A. Simpson, author of two masterly volumes on Napoleon III—the beginning of a greater undertaking which, as I was told later by his niece, he abandoned after being discouraged by an unfavorable review—and I wrote to tell him of my interest in the Second Empire and ask if I could call on him. I had no idea he was a recluse, and no doubt I was more upset than I need have been when my letter was passed on to my tutor, who summoned me to his presence and lectured me sternly about concentrating on my proper studies. As I was working very diligently, I smarted under the injustice of this attitude and never looked on my tutor, who ironically was a distinguished historian, with any degree of liking after that. Also, alas, I never met the great F. A. Simpson. Needless to say, my tutor's strictures had little effect, and I was not deterred from making an approach to another Second Empire authority, Robert Holmes Edleston, which turned out to be infinitely more productive, resulting in an enriching friendship that was to play a significant part in my development as an historian.

Being given his address by a bookseller, I wrote asking if we could meet. For some weeks there was no response, and I had almost forgotten about it when, one Sunday, the bell rang and my landlady announced that I had a caller. Waiting for me in the hall was a distinguished elderly gentleman in black who, with his short imperial, might have been the famous Duc de Morny come to life. Over the teacups in my rooms we discovered we had a strong bond in our admiration of Napoleon III. Mr. Edleston was a man of gentle charm and also—probably because I was too shy to ask him much about himself—a certain mystery. He was, as I discovered, a bachelor of private means who divided his time between his house in Cambridge and an estate in Norfolk, and owned race horses, one of which ran one year in the Grand National. In addition to his ruling passion for the French Imperial family, he was an authority on church brasses and Norfolk thoroughbreds, and on all these subjects he had written scholarly books and pamphlets which he published at his own expense. From our conversations I gained the impression that in years gone by he had haunted the hotel in the South of France where the Empress Eugénie used to stay, in order to bow respectfully as she walked through the lounge. At the sale of her possessions after her death he had bought a number of personal mementos, some of which—notably a pair of the Empress's ball slippers—came to me after he died. The front room of his house in Jesus Lane, where we had so many talks, has acquired in my memory a dreamlike quality; I see it now in the falling light of a winter's afternoon, with the large oil painting of Napoleon III lit by the soft glow of an oil lamp, for there was no gas laid on in the house, let alone electricity.

During the war Mr. Edleston and I corresponded intermittently, and in one of his letters he suggested that we should collaborate on a book about Napoleon III's visits to England. The idea gave a specific direction to my interest in the Second Empire, and I took it up with enthusiasm, beginning work on it as soon as I was demobilized. It soon transpired that it would be my book alone, for my friend was too old to collaborate actively, apart from reading and commenting upon my chapters in draft. The notes he passed over to me formed a basis for the first few chapters, but there was a vast amount of new material waiting for me in the British Museum, the Royal Library at Windsor and elsewhere, and a letter in the *Sunday Times* elicited an avalanche of replies, some of which disclosed information that had hitherto been known only within a restricted family circle. Writing this book proved to be a most rewarding experience, for I discovered I had been led to an aspect of Napoleon III's life that had not been adequately investigated before. Even reputable historians confused events that had taken place during different visits to England. It was my plan to write a detailed and accurate chronicle of these visits—from the early ones as a pretender whose claims were not taken very seriously, to those he made to Queen Victoria during his reign as Emperor, including a formal State Visit, and finally the sad last years of exile after his disastrous defeat in the Franco-Prussian War—and to show him as a staunch friend of the country that had given him shelter and a man ahead of his time whose policies foreshadowed the *entente cordiale*. His relationship with Queen Victoria, whom he fascinated in much the same way as, later, did Disraeli, was the highlight of the book, being described largely in the Queen's own words, quoted from her diaries, which I was allowed to consult in the Royal Library at Windsor. I could hardly have had a better initiation into the discipline of historical research than this project. Not only was there a vast amount of factual detail to absorb and arrange, but a close familiarity with the political and social life of the period was demanded. I spent many hours reading the basic literature, combing books of memoirs and working my way through old newspapers. This last task was specially rewarding, for my burrowings in the British Museum's Newspaper Library enabled me to acquire a knowledge of the newspaper and magazine press of London and Paris that was to be one of the main foundation stones of my future research. And it was not out of idle curiosity that, as I was scanning the columns of small print for information about Napoleon III, I paused every now and then to note a review of a ballet performance!

I completed the book in 1948 and, like many other neophyte authors, experienced difficulty in interesting a publisher in it. It was eventually brought out, as *Napoleon III in England,* by a small company run by a friend and fellow Second Empire enthusiast, W. H. Holden, who was at that time writing a biography of Cora Pearl, the celebrated *demimondaine.* Bill and I met frequently at the British Museum, and he soon became a family friend. He was a bachelor with a sort of Walter Mitty image of himself as a Second Empire *boulevardier* mixing with other young bloods and the notorious courtesans of the time, but obsessed though he was with the *demimonde,* this interest was, I am sure, entirely academic. He was what would now be termed a "loner," living, it seemed, very contentedly in a bed-sitting room. He once produced a fiancée, whom I remember as a very intelligent and elegant woman, but the engagement was very soon broken off and I was not aware of any other serious female attachment during the years I knew him. His family had intended him to go into the Army, and after leaving school he had gone to Sandhurst to be trained as a regular officer. However, although his trim figure gave him the appearance of a soldier, he left Sandhurst before completing the course, and, when I knew him, was happily spending his days doing research for his book on Cora Pearl. He must have had some private means, for he resuscitated a small publishing company he had formed before the war to publish his own book and, under an expense-sharing arrangement, my *Napoleon III in England.* He followed these two titles with several others, including a collection entitled *Second Empire Medley,* for which I wrote a piece on the cancan, but none of them turned out to be a best-seller and after a year or two his business went into liquidation. Bill's last years were sad. He had obviously gone through most of his capital, for he moved rooms frequently, each time to more modest quarters. He then contracted Parkinson's disease and spent the last few months of his life in the Home for Incurables in Putney, where he had the pleasure of discovering that a fellow patient, by name of Parrott, had been the Empress Eugénie's chauffeur. He died in Putney in 1963. His sister, the novelist Inez Holden, invited my mother and myself to a requiem mass at the Brompton Oratory which we duly attended, but it seemed to be just an ordinary service and there was no mention of Bill's name nor any sign of Inez. We never unraveled that mystery.

The collapse of Bill's publishing company meant that the unsold stock of my book was remaindered. However, I had achieved the status of a published author, and if the book made me no money, I at least had the satisfaction of seeing it become not only a rarity but also a recognized authority, frequently cited by later historians. And to my great satisfaction it saw print while Mr. Edleston, to whom it was dedicated, was still alive.

Napoleon III had not been absorbing all my literary endeavors. I was still bewitched by the Paris Opéra, and my debut in the field of dance history had taken place at the end of 1946. Having become a regular reader of Richard Buckle's magazine *Ballet,* I decided on an impulse to write up what I had discovered about the creation of *Coppélia* before someone else had the same idea. One evening I dashed off a 2,000-word article and posted it to the editor the next day with some photographs to be used for illustrations. It was accepted, and early in December 1946 I had the thrill of seeing my work in print. Success quite went to my head. The ten guineas I received seemed untold wealth, and I hurriedly wrote another article—this time on the Bal Mabille, one of the most popular dancing gardens in Paris during the 1860s.

This second article produced an invitation to lunch, from which my friendship with Dicky Buckle dates. He seems to have changed little in appearance since those days, when he sported the standard dress of an ex-Guards officer, a dark suit of impeccable cut and a bowler hat. My visits to his office in Frith Street, Soho, which he shared with his pleasant, long-suffering secretary, Miss Newman, gave me my first introduction into the world of ballet, and I began to meet critics, photographers and dancers. It was there that I first met Peter Williams, who acted as deputy for Dicky when he was away and a few years later founded *Dance and Dancers.* Later Dicky edited *Ballet* from his home in Bloomfield Terrace, Pimlico, where one morning shortly after my *Napoleon III in England* was published I arrived to find two young men sitting on the edge of the sofa, talking earnestly about ballet. They were introduced to me as Clive Barnes and John Percival of the Oxford University Ballet Club. After a few words Dicky dismissed them from his presence with the grandiloquent announcement: "Now you must leave us. Ivor Guest has come from Imperial Chislehurst and we are going to lunch to talk about Napoleon III."

I suppose I established some sort of reputation during the years I was writing for *Ballet,* even though I had produced no book on dance history, but I am sure it was less than I imagined at the time! I was very ambitious for recognition, and inwardly felt jealously antagonistic—a sign of insecurity—whenever an historical article written by anyone else appeared. It was this ambition, not the money—for the halcyon days when the magazine was flush enough to pay its contributors soon passed—that drove me to produce a steady stream of articles and to become the most prolific contributor after Dicky himself and Cyril Beaumont. Some of my articles contained the seeds of later and more substantial work. My reading of social memoirs, for instance, had revealed information about Fanny Elssler which inspired a series of articles on the dancer and her friends and sowed the first seeds of the biography I was to write many years later. An article on Clara Webster was to lead to another book, and a description of the *Pas de Quatre,* drawn from newspaper reports of the time, formed the basis of chapters in my *Romantic Ballet in England* and *Fanny Cerrito.* Among the articles which have not been incorporated in later works were a study of an unperformed ballet devised during the heyday of Romanticism by Charles Babbage, inventor of the analytical engine, and an essay on the celebrated French stage designer, Pierre Ciceri.

During this time I was not neglecting my legal studies, but for a young man who cared little for socializing and did not participate in any sport, there was ample time to indulge liberally in an increasingly obsessional avocation. Most of my evenings were my own, and after dinner I would sit down at my writing table with a fresh mind to tackle a task that was very different from the problems that occupied me during the day. As for the weekends, they were most profitably employed: Sundays gave me long stretches of time in the solitude of my study—or partial solitude, for the faithful Tiko, a black miniature poodle, slept peacefully at my side—while Saturdays were reserved for research at the British Museum.

Carefully and methodically undertaken, this research was to provide me with a bedrock of data on which most of the work I have done since has to some degree been based. My field of investigation was originally limited in place and time—the Paris of the Second Empire—and I worked through all the Parisian newspapers of that time that were to be found in the British Museum Newspaper Library at Colindale. I soon realized I was excavating virgin soil, as I turned up engravings of scenes from ballets and caricatures of dancers that, almost inexplicably, had lain undetected for nearly a hundred years. Reading eyewitness accounts of performances, written in the vividly descriptive style of the time, I acquired an extensive knowledge not only of the ballets and dancers of a century before, but also of the inner workings of the Opéra. Théophile Gautier was, of course, my chief guide, but there were other critics who emerged from the pages of old newspapers to add to my understanding—notably Pier-Angelo Fiorentino, a Neapolitan who enjoyed special contacts with the ballet and interlaced his notices with inside information and valuable technical details. At about the same time I began to work through the London press of the Romantic period, beginning with *The Times,* building up a day-by-day chronicle of ballet in England that I was later to enrich from other newspapers and periodicals.

For the theatre historian the daily press is an essential source. If reliable light is to be shed on a period of theatre history, there is no substitute for the plodding hard work that is involved in assembling basic information, for it is only through direct and exhaustive familiarity with contemporary material and the ability to make a balanced personal assessment that one can hope to re-create the past without distortion. There are, of course, other qualities that are indispensable in a ballet historian: an understanding of activities and trends in other branches of the theatre, a mastery of the social scene, familiarity with the literature and art of the period, and of music and how composers regarded writing for the ballet, and the directions in which the thought of the time was moving. Because of these many facets, and because every age views history in a different perspective, there can perhaps be no such thing as the ideal dance historian or the definitive dance history.

When I entered the field of dance history, my paramount objective was to achieve a detailed reconstruction of the past—in short, to bring it to life for the reader. My imagination was so stirred that no detail was too unimportant not to be fitted into the mosaic I wanted to create by my writing. Indeed, it was this very lack of detail which marred for me so much of the historical writing on the ballet I had then read. Later my views became somewhat more tolerant, and I accepted that not every writer has the ability or the perseverance to assemble and marshal facts, and that there are some whose strength lies more in the perception of ideas and trends. In my own case I possess the former quality in greater strength than the latter, and it gives me satisfaction to see my works providing the factual basis for writers who are more concerned with interpreting the developments I have chronicled.

During the winter of 1948–49 I had to prepare for my final law examination, and I disciplined myself to renounce all writing for six months. My only concession was to reserve Saturdays for work at the British Museum. At that time I was still trying to place my book on Napoleon III, and I put it in the hands of a literary agent who had a small office in the Strand. I soon came to see I had made a poor choice. Both in appearance and manner he reminded me of a book-

maker, and I finally lost my confidence when, on my casually re-
marking that my next book was to be about the ballet, he jovially
urged me to give it plenty of spice—"a touch of the light fantastic,
you know." I lost no time in retrieving my manuscript from his
philistine hands, and ever since then I have always dealt directly
with publishers.

The feeling of release which came over me when I arrived home
after sitting my last paper for the Law Society's final examination
was exhilarating. I went at once to my desk and began writing *The
Ballet of the Second Empire* from the vast quantity of notes that had
accumulated in my files. There was still much research to do. As the
work took shape, gaps appeared that had to be filled—here background needed to be built up, here a passage called for elaboration,
there a clue emerged to be followed up—and the list of questions to
be taken with me on my next visit to Paris grew.

Being at that time unmarried and unattached, I was able to indulge
my eccentric whim and for nearly fifteen years to spend my holidays
in Paris, devoting weeks on end to dedicated research among archives and collections which I was beginning to know intimately.
Photocopying facilities, where they were available at all, were very
primitive—the Xerox was not then invented—and passages had to
be laboriously copied by hand. Much of my time was spent methodically and painstakingly working through periodicals—notably the
daily theatrical papers such as the *Courrier des Spectacles* and
L'Entr'acte—and the boxes containing contracts, correspondence
and records of ballets produced at the Opéra.

I continued to receive the warmest of welcomes at the Library of
the Opéra, where I was treated as a member of the family and allowed into nooks and crannies of the building which were not accessible to the ordinary reader. This was a most precious privilege. One
of the sanctums to which I was admitted was known as Salle X.
This was situated on the eastern side of the building, and in the early
days of the Palais Garnier had housed the Library. When I knew it,
it was still used for storage. Shelves were weighted down by brown-
paper packages of orchestral parts, all sorts of odd memorabilia
were scattered about—I once came across the director's desk diaries
for the 1860s—and up a short flight of steps were cabinets filled
with drawings, designs and maquettes, all at that time uncata-
logued. It was there that I discovered, among other treasures in a
drawer labeled "Fond Taglioni," the greater part of the model for
the second act setting of *La Sylphide,* which I had photographed and
published with a short note in *Ballet.*

Another voyage of discovery was with Jean Corday, the retired archivist, who led me to a room where scores of portraits were stacked. There, as if waiting for me, begrimed and damaged, was Laure's portrait of Fanny Cerrito. We took it down to the Library, Mme. Morillon's husband skilfully repaired and cleaned it, and ever since it has occupied a place of honor in the Museum.

I completed the manuscript of *The Ballet of the Second Empire* towards the end of 1950. With some hesitation I asked Cyril Beaumont if he would do me the honor of reading it. I had, of course, been a customer at his bookshop in the Charing Cross Road for some years, and as my articles began to appear in *Ballet,* I found myself invited into the little dark room at the back where he sat at a small table overflowing with a seemingly disorganized mountain of paper that rose up around his portable typewriter. I soon discovered that, in spite of appearances, he knew exactly where everything was on that table! Once when he needed his pen, which I alone could see peeping out from the papers on my side of the table, he stretched out his hand and unerringly grasped it. I left my manuscript with him, expecting him to return it with a few general comments after a week or two, but I found myself invited to a series of hour-long discussions around lunchtime when he would go through one or two chapters at a time—never more—correcting a technical point here, suggesting a rephrasing there, and literally weighing up every word. This generosity toward a virtually unknown writer made a deep impression on me, and in my turn I have endeavored to repay it by helping younger historians.

It was Beaumont who introduced me to Cyril Swinson of A. & C. Black, the leading publishers of books on ballet. "Swin" was to become one of my closest friends. He was a significant figure in the ballet scene, whose contribution to dance literature is today largely overlooked. Singlehandedly he built up Blacks' celebrated "ballet list," which began in 1936 with Arnold Haskell's *Balletomane's Scrapbook* and continued until the last issue of *Ballet Annual* shortly before his death in 1963. No other publisher can have fathered so many books on the dance as Swin, who to most of his authors became also friend, counselor and inspirer. When I delivered my manuscript and the collection of more than four hundred photographs I had amassed, he brought me down to earth by warning me that he would have difficulty in convincing his directors—he was not then on the Board himself—that such a specialized work would be a viable publishing proposition. But he persevered on my behalf and after more than two years accomplished the "breakthrough'' with the formula of bringing it out in two parts, with no commitment being made for the second part until it was seen how the first had been received. The logical procedure would have been to publish the first five chapters first, but faced with the possibility that the second part might never come out, I asked that the first volume should comprise the last five chapters. These included the two chapters which meant most to me: those on Emma Livry and *Coppélia.* Happily the first volume pleased the critics, and two years later Blacks brought out the rest of the work.

As it was my first book on ballet history, I have a special affection for *The Ballet of the Second Empire,* which gave me greater pleasure in the writing than any of my other works. It was a product of my obsession with its period at its most intense. For years before I had been accumulating a vast store of knowledge about Paris life of that time from the daily routine of the palace to the social round and the everyday activities and pleasures of ordinary people, from the music heard at concerts to the popular tunes to which people danced, and even down to such details as the price of cabs and the omnibus routes! In my daydreams I could almost imagine myself transported back to those times, and the world of the dancers at the Opéra was particularly vivid. On another level, it was for me a happy coincidence that the Second Empire had been almost totally overlooked in histories of ballet, for nothing is more satisfying to a historian than to find himself working in virgin soil. Further, the neglect of this period by the historians led me to realize there were other gaps in what was, of course, a continuing developing process.

The basic plan of *The Ballet of the Second Empire* was a straightforward chronicle, dealing with each new ballet and important revival and touching on changes in the hierarchy of the ballet company and the administrative structure of the Paris Opéra and other events affecting French ballet as they occurred. This chronicle was preceded by an introductory chapter, which I wrote last of all, explaining the significance of the period in ballet history and generally presenting the background to the main narrative—the structure of the ballet company and the school, the system of examinations, society's attitude towards the dancer, and the work of the critics whose reviews are the basis of so much of our present knowledge. Later I was to adopt the same plan when writing the companion work, *The Romantic Ballet in Paris,* and I shall probably do so again in the book I hope to write in due time on the Paris ballet during the period of the French Revolution and the First Empire.

In the hope that my book would become the standard work of

reference on the subject, I included at the end a number of tables. These comprised lists of the principal ballet masters, the *régisseurs de la danse,* the teachers of the perfection class, and the principal dancers, all with relevant dates. Then came a list of the ballet creations at the Opéra, with dates of first performance, names of choreographer, scenarist, composer, designers and the principal dancers, number of performances and the time it survived in the repertory, and the average receipts over the first ten performances. This was followed by a list of divertissements arranged for operas. Lastly I compiled a list of dance activities at the other Parisian theatres that was as complete as my careful perusal of the press for the period could make it. In these appendices were to be found most of the basic factual information that any student might require. Originally I planned to add another appendix, containing poems inspired by dancers of the time, but this had to be sacrificed for commercial reasons.

Very few readers noticed an amusing error in the first edition. One of the books I had consulted was Newman's classic biography of Wagner, and by an aberration of the mind I listed the author's first name in the bibliography not as Ernest, but as Bernard! Within a few days I received a postcard from that great balletomane and corrector, Lionel Bradley, pointing out the mistake, but only one reviewer—the late Ifan Kyrle Fletcher—was observant enough to notice it.

While Swin was working on his directors in his unflagging endeavors to persuade them to accept this book, he would occasionally suggest that I might try another publisher in the interval before the next meeting of the Board. It was during one such interval that I approached John Baker, managing director of Phoenix House, who was anxious to add some ballet titles to his list. As it happened, I could not arouse his interest in my Second Empire book, but I persuaded him to commission me to write a book on the Romantic ballet in London. Much of the groundwork I had already done, and the shape of the book dictated itself. It did not break new ground in quite the same way as my Second Empire book. Both Mark Perugini and Cyril Beaumont had written on the Romantic ballet before the war, and the American periodical, *Dance Index,* had produced an issue by George Chaffee, "The Romantic Ballet in London," which marked an important advance as a work of scholarship. However, even this last work had only skimmed the contemporary sources. It seemed amazing to me that no one had investigated the daily press beyond *The Times* and the *Illustrated London News,* for in my visits to the British Museum Newspaper Library I had discovered that there was a wealth of material in other papers and journals of the time. In particular, the *Morning Post* and the *Morning Herald* contained vivid descriptions of ballet performances, and, on a lighter note, some of the scurrilous papers of the early Victorian era, such as the *Satirist,* revealed intimate details of the relations of dancers with the world of fashionable society.

The *Romantic Ballet in England,* which was published in 1954, was written to a more general plan than my Second Empire study. I aimed to give a broad survey of the period, linking it to the years that had led up to it and highlighting a number of salient subjects from the work of important choreographers and significant ballets to side issues such as visits of Spanish dancers and a frivolous chapter on a backstage scandal. One of the most important chapters, to my mind, was an account of early performances of *Giselle* in London, in which I drew attention—incredibly, for the first time—to Fanny Elssler's notable interpretation. The book was given a flattering reception, but was rightly criticized by Cyril Beaumont for not containing an examination of Romanticism as it affected ballet, a shortcoming which I endeavored to remedy in a new introduction which I wrote for the second edition.

CHAPTER THREE

Fanny and Clara

FEW love affairs can have had such a bizarre beginning as my passion for Fanny Cerrito. It took hold of me as I searched for the date of her death, which I needed for one of the appendices to my *Ballet of the Second Empire.* I had had little difficulty in discovering when and where most of the principal dancers of that time had died, and had arrived at the annoying situation where only one—and she one of the greatest, Cerrito—eluded me.

True, the *Complete Book of Ballets* gave the place and date of her death as Switzerland in 1899, but I suspected, correctly as it transpired, that Cyril Beaumont had confused Cerrito with Carlotta Grisi. Refusing to admit defeat, I embarked on a quest that lasted eighteen months and occupied many days of my time before I was rewarded at last with the information I sought . . . and much more besides.

The search entailed many hours scanning the pages of old newspapers, a task that is inevitably slow (though not tedious, for one is constantly being distracted by some fascinating news item that is quite irrelevant to one's main purpose) and, after a concentrated spell of several hours, tiring on the eyes. For a time the latest information I had that Cerrito was alive was Arthur Pougin's statement, in an encyclopedia article published in 1890, that she was then "living in retirement in Paris." Then further delving in the newspapers *Le Figaro* and *Le Gaulois* revealed a brief reference that she was still alive in 1898. On and on I plodded in search of an announcement of her death, but without any result. Had she died outside France, I wondered. Almost in desperation I directed my attention to Italian papers, caused enquiries to be made in Switzerland (in case Beaumont had been correct after all), and even searched the registers of deaths at Somerset House in London, but all to no avail.

These frustrations only strengthened my determination to track Cerrito down, and I found myself absorbed by a new challenge and a new ambition. Cerrito, the ballerina whom the London audiences took to their hearts more than any other dancer, had been ignored by biographers, and I resolved to remedy that lack myself. In the first flush of enthusiasm I drafted a specimen chapter, choosing as my theme the drama of her first appearance at Her Majesty's Theatre in 1840, which had to be postponed because of the famous "Tamburini row," when demonstrators invaded the stage and brought the performance to an abrupt close. It had been amusingly described in one of the *Ingoldsby Legends:*

> Then all the gentle folks flew in a rage,
> And they jumped from the Omnibus on to the Stage,
> Lords, Squires and Knights, they came down to the lights,
> In their opera-hats, and their opera tights.
> Ma'am'selle Cherrytoes shook to her very toes,
> She couldn't hop on, so hopp'd off on her merry toes.

I had reached this state of enthusiasm when Lolita de Pedroso came into my life. Lolita comes from a noble Spanish family, and the friendship between our two families had begun before the First World War, when my mother had finished her education at Dieudonne, a small and very exclusive school near Paris owned and run by Lolita's grandmother, the Marquesa de San Carlos de Pedroso. For some years my mother had lost touch with the Pedrosos, but the thread was providentially picked up again in 1949 after she had joined me on one of my visits to Paris and we had searched for the San Carlos family tomb in the Montmartre Cemetery, dreading that we might discover they were all dead and buried. Mercifully our fears were not realized, and old friendships were renewed. And in the summer of 1950 Lolita wrote to ask if she could spend a few weeks with us in Chislehurst.

Of all my friends, Lolita is the most unusual. Instead of devoting her life to the conventional fashionable round, she embarked on an adventurous existence that took her as a war correspondent to Abyssinia, brought her into the center of momentous events in the Spanish Civil War, and led her to the great passion of her life—the dance. She is to be counted among those cultured aficionados who have supported, advised and inspired dancers and acted as indispensable catalysts in the evolution of the art. An invitation from the Royal Academy of Dancing to give a lecture-demonstration on Spanish dancing at Covent Garden had brought her to England, and she had sought our hospitality totally unaware that I was in any way involved with the ballet.

Naturally a strong bond united us from the very beginning of our friendship, and she became the first person to read the trial chapter I had written on Fanny Cerrito. One evening at dinner an unusual opportunity of tracing this elusive ballerina's death presented itself. We were discussing psychic phenomena, and Lolita told us of a friend in Madrid who had a contact with the spirit world in the form of a ballet dancer who, most unusually, materialized from head to toe and even sat on his knee! Almost facetiously I suggested that her friend's medium was in an excellent position to find out when and where Cerrito had died. Lolita seemed willing to ask, but when she returned to Madrid, she felt qualms about broaching such a delicate subject and of course I understood, although I was naturally disappointed. It would have been a unique feat to have obtained the information from "the other side."

That July, when I was in Paris, I attended a ceremony at the Montmartre Cemetery, where the tomb of Auguste Vestris had been restored through the initiative of Serge Lifar. I also paid a visit to my friend, Olive Abbott, an English lady who had worked in Paris for many years as a secretary and on retirement had taken up historical research. I had been introduced to her by Bill Holden, and from time to time she had undertaken odd tasks for me at the incredible rate of 2s. 6d. (12½ p. or 24¢) an hour. She was vastly entertaining, and I spent several happy evenings dining with her in her little *pavillon* behind the Avenue de Neuilly and listening to her reminiscences. She could recall the fire at the Bal de la Charité, and had had many interesting experiences during the Second World War. Being English, she was continually under suspicion, but she proved a match for the Gestapo and her concierge, and gave shelter to a succession of escaping airmen on their perilous journeys back to England. In appearance she was the Frenchman's caricature of an Englishwoman, with a long nose and prominent teeth, and an outrageous English accent. I had already enlisted her support in my search for Cerrito's death, and for more than a year she had been following up such clues as I could give her. Now she told me that there was just one more avenue to explore, and that if nothing came of that, I might just as well give up.

The final clue I had provided was the address of a house in Paris which Cerrito had owned in the 1870s, and Miss Abbott had written to the Archivist of the Enregistrement Domaine et Timbre. Within a week of my return to England my search was at an end. Eureka! Miss Abbott wrote to tell me the Archivist had given her the information I wanted: Cerrito had died at her home at No. 2 rue Théry on May 6th, 1909. And a few days later she wrote again, telling me that Cerrito's tomb was in the Montmartre Cemetery—not fifty yards from where I had been standing a few weeks before at the Vestris ceremony.

Miss Abbott was indefatigable. She then proceeded to cultivate an official at the Ministry of Finance and from him ascertained the name of Cerrito's notary. Notarial practices in France are handed down from one holder to another, and she called on the successor who obligingly searched out the Will from his archives and read it out to her. At first reading it did not sound very exciting: a few small legacies to servants, a nephew and a cousin, and the residue left to a Madame d'Acuña of Madrid.

The mention of Madrid set me writing to Lolita. Would it be possible, I asked, to trace a Mme. d'Acuña, presumably a friend of Cerrito, who inherited her modest estate more than forty years before? I did not know that Acuña was a fairly common name, but researcher's luck was with me. Within a few days I had Lolita's reply, one of the most exciting communications I have ever received.

"I have already made enquiries about Cerrito," she wrote, "and I think I may have some interesting news for you." What a masterly understatement this was! "I wondered at first how to begin finding out; it all seemed rather like a puzzle. After thinking things over with Arno" . . . this was Arno Dosch-Fleurot, the celebrated journalist, who was a close friend . . . "and consulting the lady of my house whose sister is very much in the international set, I was able to get some quite extraordinary data! To begin with, the name of Mme. d'Acuña's husband is Lebreton. This Lebreton happens to be the father of an old friend of my people in Madrid. And Mme. d'Acuña, his wife, was . . . just guess Ivor! Well, she was a daughter Cerrito had by the Marques de Bedmar, a Spanish aristocrat."

This development was so incredible that I felt sure it was preordained. Lolita followed up the lead and made contact with Cerrito's granddaughter who, although married to a grandee, turned out to be most cooperative. A visit to Madrid was essential, and in 1953 I had the moving experience of meeting the Marquesa de Villadarias and her daughter who, though she had heavier features, bore a marked resemblance to the ballerina.

By the Marquesa and another relative I was privileged to be given a vivid insight into Cerrito's old age, and was allowed to reproduce a wonderful collection of portraits, drawings and photographs that had remained in the possession of the family, almost as if waiting for me. My biography would have been very much poorer if I had not so fortuitously located Cerrito's descendants. The Marquesa wrote to me every Christmas until her death. One year she sent me a photograph of herself and her grandmother, and in 1964 I received, instead of the usual Christmas card, a gift that touched me more than I can ever express—the original watercolor by de Valentini of Cerrito in the ballet *Alma*. "I am charging my dear grandmother," the Marquesa wrote in her covering note, "to bring you and your wife my Christmas wishes. I am very old, and feel that this charming portrait will be happier in your hands, you who have said so many kind things about her."

I find it all too easy to be carried away by my exciting memories of tracing Cerrito's family, and to forget the days and days of laborious research that were needed to build up a rounded and detailed account of a career that was played out in more than a score of opera houses. For the London seasons, which were of prime importance because of the roles created for her there by Jules Perrot, I was on my home ground, and the rich collection of newspapers at the British Museum yielded a plethora of contemporary accounts from which I was able to create—at least in my own mind—a clear idea of how she must have danced. I was no less familiar with the French material, which I had already gathered for *The Ballet of the Second Empire*. But Cerrito had danced in many other cities—in Vienna, throughout Italy, in Madrid, St. Petersburg, Moscow—and all these had to be covered. At the time I was very conscious that I could not cover these areas so thoroughly as London and Paris, and in later works such as my biographies of Elssler and Zucchi I have endeavored to rectify this.

Unless a theatre historian is free to devote all his time to unremunerative work—and thorough research of this sort is essentially unremunerative—and can himself visit archives, libraries and museums in other cities all over the world and gather the material without need of assistants or translators, he must do some of his research at one remove, by finding reliable research workers to work at his direction. It takes time to accumulate contacts, and this is, alas, a continuing process because such contacts are often retired folk who, being mortal, are prone to disappear.

In Vienna I was fortunate in finding Bertha Niederle, a distinguished theatre historian in her own right, who was perfectly familiar with the sources which I was required to consult and who combed them with great thoroughness. There was not a great deal to cover for Cerrito, but happily I had the foresight to set her working on Fanny Elssler, and over a period of years she sent me a vast quantity of meticulously assembled notes and microfilm which I was to use when writing my biography of the latter ballerina. Later, in 1962, my wife and I had tea with her when we were in Vienna on our honeymoon, but she died shortly afterwards, before I began to write my book on Elssler.

Italy presents special problems to the dance historian because there were so many centers of theatrical activity, and dancers toured the peninsula, often visiting several cities in a single year. The history of Italian ballet is very fragmented and still awaits the historian with the background knowledge, patience and skill to produce a homogeneous study. For my biography of Cerrito I was able to consult contemporary newspapers of Milan and Naples in the British Museum, and a rare theatrical periodical, published in Bologna, at the University Library, Cambridge. I was also familiar with the Silvestri collection of Italian ballet scenarios at the Paris Opéra. But more than this was needed to give the Italian sections of my book sufficient weight to balance the detail in the English chapters. Cerrito was a Neapolitan, and I found, first of all, a theatre historian from Naples, Professor Ulisse Proto-Giurleo, with whom I had an entertaining correspondence and who traced Cerrito's birth and revealed that she had consistently subtracted four years from her age!

But the friend who taught me most about the sources for the history of Italian ballet was Walter Toscanini, son of the maestro and a close friend of Lillian Moore. It was Walter who opened the doors of the Museo alla Scala for me, and gave me an introduction to its director, Stefano Vittadini, who obligingly had the reviews of Cerrito's performances at La Scala, published in the Milanese theatrical journals, microfilmed for me. When the book was finished, Walter read through the manuscript and suggested a number of additions that greatly enriched it. We did not meet until 1962, when my wife and I dined at his New York mansion on Riverside Drive and were shown his incredible archives—part devoted to the work of his father, and part to the history of Italian ballet, on which he was an authority without a peer. Sadly, the book he was preparing was never completed, for not long after we met he suffered a disabling stroke from which he never recovered, but his manuscript was used by Marian Hannah Winter for her magistral *Pre-Romantic Ballet*. His dance materials are now available to scholars at the Dance Collection of The New York Public Library.

Where my book was weakest was in the chapter on Cerrito's two seasons at the end of her career in Russia. I had not then forged the contacts that were to enable me to describe in detail the Russian seasons of Elssler and Zucchi, and the chapter was based on what books and newspapers I could consult in London. Were I ever to revise this book, it is that chapter above all that I would wish to rewrite and expand.

The boom in ballet books was slackening when my manuscript was ready to be submitted to a publisher, and I feared it might be a difficult book to place. But John Baker of Phoenix House agreed to publish it, and produced a very handsome volume, graced with a colored frontispiece showing Cerrito dancing the famous *pas de l'ombre*.

I dedicated the book to Paulette Dynalix, whose sensitive performance of the travesty role of Frantz in *Coppélia* at the Paris Opéra had been the starting point of our friendship, and she was the guest of honor at the publication party which my cousins, Michael and Odile Tweedie, gave for me in their apartment in the Avenue Marceau. Paulette had a long and distinguished career at the Opéra, and only narrowly missed being nominated *étoile*. In her late teens, just before the war, she had been one of the three young dancers who competed for the role of Giselle—the others were Darsonval and Didion—and, knowing her sensitive feeling for character, I have often regretted that I never saw her in this role, which at the time she was the youngest dancer ever to have performed at the Opéra. We had been introduced, in 1950, at a lecture which Lifar gave at the Library of the Opéra, and she provided me with an insight into the dancers' life at the Opéra which, I am sure, has greatly sharpened my understanding of its history. She now has, in her own library, a unique item—the original manuscript of *Fanny Cerrito*.

My next book was *Victorian Ballet-girl*, a short study of the young English dancer, Clara Webster, who was fatally burned on the stage of Drury Lane in 1844. Hers had been a short life, and if her career was only on the point of flowering at the end, she was already being recognized as an English dancer of extraordinary promise in an age dominated by foreign stars. But of her private life virtually nothing was known, and what she was like as a person was likely to remain a mystery. It was impossible, therefore, to write a biography in the strict sense, and so I decided to intertwine her career with a description of the ballet girl's life at that time and an account of the dangers of fire that dancers then had to face.

I first had to ascertain exactly where Clara fitted into the genealogical tree of the famous theatrical family of the Websters. My attention was drawn to Bath by a statement in a contemporary newspaper that she was closely related to the theatre manager, Benjamin Webster, who according to the *Dictionary of National Biography* was born there. This proved to be a good lead, and a search in the parish registers in and around the city enabled me to verify the genealogy and correct the Webster family tree in *Who's Who in the Theatre*. Next I had to reconstruct Clara's career from playbills and old newspapers. Her career proved to be astonishingly long for one so young, for she had gone into the theatre at a very early age. By a painstaking search through the provincial press I followed her from Bath to Swansea, back to Bath again, to London, to Dublin, to Liverpool and Manchester, and then to London again, where she seemed at the threshold of an important career when the tragedy occurred.

At the end of all the spadework that was needed to present her life story I was rewarded with another breakthrough that brought me close to my subject. It happened as a result of a letter which Lillian Moore found in the Harvard Theatre Collection—apparently the only autograph of Clara Webster to survive. It was a note to the manager of Drury Lane, Alfred Bunn, written just a week before the accident, saying she was too ill to appear that night. On the letter Bunn had added the caustic comment: ". . . on which night she was in perfect health and out with Mr. Michael Bruce (Grenadier Guards) at the Tilt Yard!!!"

Who was this Michael Bruce? Army Lists revealed he became a General, and *Burke's Landed Gentry* disclosed he had two grandsons living, one a Canon of the Church of England and the other a Brigadier. I thought it wise to opt for the Brigadier, and my carefully worded letter brought a delightful reply and an invitation to lunch. It turned out Brigadier Ian Bruce had just written a book about Lady Hester Stanhope's affair with his great-grandfather, so he was not in the slightest offended by my investigation of a scandalous incident in his family history. In fact, I was able to tell him more than he could tell me, for I had unearthed a number of *on dit* paragraphs from the *Satirist*, but he lent me two pathetic letters which his grandfather had received in later life from one of Clara's colleagues in the *corps de ballet* who had fallen on hard times.

Not wishing to leave even a tombstone unturned, I wrote to Kensal Green cemetery to enquire if Clara's grave still existed, and received this reply: "The coffin containing the remains of Clara Vestris Webster . . . is still deposited in Public Vault 21 Catacomb E and the registered number of the deposit is 4394. Apparently no Mausoleum has been erected in the Cemetery but if it is intended to have such a Mausoleum built I shall be pleased to deal with your enquiry." Maybe one of these days someone will form a Clara Webster Society and erect a suitable monument. Meanwhile I decided, a little immodestly perhaps, that I would let my book be my contribution to her memory!

Giuseppina Bozzacchi, the first Swanilda. Photo: Reutlinger.

Above: Ivor Guest at the Library of the Paris Opéra in 1952, with Serge Lifar, François Guillot de Rode, Jacques Feschotte, Françoise Adret and Anatole Chujoy. Photo: Max Erlanger de Rosen.

Left: The Library of the Paris Opéra. Georges Clairin's portrait of Virginia Zucchi looks down on the readers. Photo: Michel Szabo.

Left: Ivor Guest and Lillian Moore in Bickley, Spring 1961.

Below: Emma Livry in *le Papillon*. Biscuit china statuette by Auguste Barre. Photo: G.B.L. Wilson.

The Laure portrait of Fanny Cerrito, rediscovered by Ivor Guest at the Paris Opéra.

The Model for Act II of *La Sylphide* — another discovery by Ivor Guest at the Opéra.

The Editorial Board of *Ballet Annual* entertaining Beryl Grey in 1952. From left to right: Arnold Haskell, Beryl Grey, Cyril Swinson, Ivor Guest, Mary Clarke, G.B.L. Wilson. Photo: G.B.L. Wilson.

To Two—
with best—
... from
Spanish
friend
Lolita
1953

Above: The Christmas gift from Fanny Cerrito's granddaughter. De Valentini's painting of Cerrito in *Alma*.

Left: Lolita de Pedroso. Photo by Baron.

At the Fanny Cerrito publication party, 1956. Left to right: Odile Tweedie, the hostess, Paulette Dynalix, Rita Thalia, Ivor Guest. Photo: Max Erlanger de Rosen.

Adeline Genée, c. 1955.

CHAPTER FOUR

Adeline Genée

A MEETING with Adeline Genée had a certain similarity to a presentation at Court. One received a summons. Invariably the venue for the audience was the Hyde Park Hotel, a massive monument to Edwardian comfort where she resided during her visits to London, and it was there, in the corner she made her own, that I met her for the first time early in 1955. She had retired from the presidency of the Royal Academy of Dancing the year before, and I had chosen to write an article about her for the next *Ballet Annual*. P. J. S. Richardson, doyen of writers on the dance and a friend of hers of long standing, told me I ought to meet her and arrange a lunch party. I recall feeling very much in awe when I was presented, but I quickly fell under the spell of her prim but nonetheless warm personality.

My article must have pleased her, for a year later I received a summons. "Dear Mr. Guest," she wrote (I was never to be addressed differently, and indeed I believe Anton Dolin alone among her friends in the ballet world was permitted to be on Christian name terms with her), "Will you give me the pleasure of seeing you at the Hyde Park Hotel for lunch Friday next (16th) at one o'clock? I should be very glad if you are disengaged and feel inclined to come." How strongly the fragrance of the Edwardian era, with its well-ordered rules for polite behavior, comes across in those phrases.

This time we lunched together tête-a-tête, and she quickly came to the purpose of her invitation. Would I, she asked, be prepared to write her autobiography? Anton Dolin had been working on it for several years, but he had not been able to make the progress she desired. In January 1958 she would be eighty, and she was very anxious that the publication should coincide with her birthday. This was wholly unexpected. It was, I appreciated, a most exceptional compliment she was paying me, but the proposal carried a heavy responsibility and required careful consideration. My pride as a writer rejected the idea of "ghosting," and the commitments of my legal practice and the detailed study of the French Romantic ballet, upon which I had already embarked and which I did not wish to put aside completely, made me reluctant to accept a deadline I might not be able to meet, particularly since I had no idea how much research would be involved. There was also the delicate question of taking over from Dolin. I explained these points to Genée, and told her I would be willing to write her biography under my own name, but while I would not be dilatory I could not enter into a commitment to a deadline. She realistically accepted that it was important that the writing of the book should not be unduly rushed and that it was not practicable to expect it to be published in time for her eightieth birthday, and she undertook to clear the matter with Dolin so that there would be no embarrassment there. In matters of business she was always prompt, punctilious and correct, and it took but little time to settle the arrangements between us and negotiate a contract, through Swin, with Blacks.

In writing about a subject who was still alive I was faced with a situation I had not encountered in any of my previous books. Although it had been agreed it was to be my book, I realized that I could not disregard Genée's own wishes and susceptibilities, and that this might prove to be a source of conflict, but on the other hand there was the great advantage that my subject would be available to check facts and fill in detail when required. To make the task of collecting information easier and quicker, I decided to buy a tape recorder (then still something of a novelty)—a very heavy piece of equipment which I took to the Hyde Park Hotel for our first discussion about how to work together on the book. But Genée made it very clear she did not want her conversations taped, and the machine seemed doubly heavy when, feeling unusually tired, I carried it away afterwards.

The reason for my fatigue was revealed next day when I woke to find myself covered with spots. I had come down with chicken pox! I was still feeling very ill a few mornings later when the postman brought several enormous parcels containing the material Genée had retrieved from Dolin. I groaned and turned my face to the wall, wishing I had never undertaken the task. After a few days, however, I was in a brighter mood. I began to explore the contents of the parcels, and my enthusiasm mounted. Here was a treasure trove of material. Most fascinating of all were several versions of her memoirs which she had begun at various stages of her life but never finished. There were cuttings, playbills and scenarios that told the story of the small touring company which her uncle, Alexander Genée, had run in the 1880s. Two large albums were bursting with newspaper cuttings of her own career, her American visits being covered in great detail. And most evocative of all were the scores of photographs of her, both on stage and off, from childhood days, through her career as a ballerina to her later years. All this, added to the information I had already gathered myself, made it possible to start writing almost at once.

During the weeks I was infectious I worked solidly in my study, with my faithful poodle Tiko at my side. My first task was to sort out the material and make an index so that I could instantly retrieve any item of information when required. This took a few days, after which I took up my pen and began writing the first draft. Carried away by my enthusiasm, I worked so quickly that by the time my quarantine was over, about a third of the book was sketched out.

As each chapter was drafted and typed, a copy was sent to Genée, who returned it with her comments endorsed in the margins. (This annotated copy of the first draft is now in the archives of the Royal Academy of Dancing, together with all the material I used when writing the book.) My apprehensions about possible conflicts proved unfounded, for she respected my position as author and never insisted on a change unless I had made an error of fact. We worked together very harmoniously, and I can recall only one occasion when our approaches seemed to diverge. This was when she handed me a long list of names, headed by the Duke of Newcastle and going down through the order of precedence, of friends whom she wanted mentioned in the book. I explained that the book would be primarily about her career as an artist and that, while some of the friends concerned would naturally find a place in the story, to include them all would hold up the flow of the narrative. She did not press the point, although I think she was a little disappointed, for in one of our last meetings, some time after the book was published, she said to me with a humorous twinkle: "Of course I still have to write *my* book."

Rereading the letters which Genée wrote to me when the book was on the stocks, I am forcefully reminded how involved she became. Being a stickler for detail, I would bombard her with questions, which she always answered patiently, promptly and with great precision. Sometimes she even undertook tasks of research, writing to Derra de Moroda to check details about her season in Munich, and obtaining information from Copenhagen about her visit to the Royal Theatre in 1902.

Finally, when the draft had been corrected and polished, we went through it together one last time. Every evening for nearly a fortnight we dined together at the Hyde Park Hotel, going up to her room afterwards to check the typescript, chapter by chapter, for accuracy. She would put on a green eye-shade—being very fair, she was troubled by strong light—and we would work with great concentration until it was time for me to leave and catch a late train back to Bickley. On one occasion, I remember, she looked up at about 10:30 and said to me: "Now I must send you home. You must be getting tired." There was no sign that she was wilting!

I was greatly encouraged to see her identifying herself so wholeheartedly with the book. She concerned herself even with details of production. It was at her suggestion that her monogram was embossed on the binding, and also through her that the book had a color frontispiece. She shamed the publishers into this by offering to contribute £50 herself for the additional cost, an offer that was not taken up. I think she may have expected the book to sell better than it did, for in one letter she plaintively told me it was not on display at the bookshops she had visited. Looking back on our collaboration, I feel I could not have been more fortunate in my subject, and can only hope she considered herself half as lucky in having me as her biographer.

The research I undertook for the book on Genée led to two more general studies on the music-hall era of English ballet between 1860 and the First World War, another neglected period—one on the ballet at the Alhambra Theatre, published in 1959 as *Dance Perspectives 4,* and the other on the ballet at the Empire Theatre, which was brought out in 1962 by the Society for Theatre Research. Another interesting "spin off" from the book was a 45 r.p.m. record of Genée reminiscing about her career, made by Jupiter Recordings. For this I wrote her script, and accompanied her to the studio where she recorded it well-nigh faultlessly. Of course, being a perfection-ist in all things, she had rehearsed it very thoroughly in the privacy of her room at the Hyde Park Hotel.

It was at that time that I organized an important exhibition of books on ballet for the National Book League. For the catalogue I had written brief notes to introduce the various groups of books, and the idea came to me, one day in the bath, that these might be ex-panded into a short history of ballet. There was at that time no adequate history that was both balanced and accurate, and I thought this was a need I could fill. I called on Arnold Haskell for his ad-vice, and in the course of our discussion he suggested the title—*The Dancer's Heritage*.

Writing this book was a very healthy exercise for me, forcing me to take an overall view of history after so much specialized work. My aim was to survey the history of ballet from its beginnings as an art of spectacle during the Renaissance to the present day, showing it to be a continual process of development. It was intended as no more than an introduction to the subject, presented in such a way as to catch the interest and imagination of a young reader and to en-courage him to move on to more specialized studies. Modest as were its dimensions, it was written with great care, and before publication was checked by a number of my colleagues for whose opinions I have the greatest respect.

First of these was Mary Clarke, who read each chapter as it was written. I had first met Mary in 1950 when she was a member of the team P. W. Manchester had gathered round her when she was edit-ing *Ballet Today,* and I soon appreciated her wide knowledge of the ballet, her balanced judgment, and her fluent style as a writer. I can proudly boast of having nudged Cyril Swinson into commissioning her to write a history of the Sadler's Wells Ballet, and when this book, now the standard work on the early years of our national ballet, was published in 1955, Mary inscribed my copy, "For Ivor—who was really responsible for the whole thing." That was one of the most warming compliments I have ever received. We both joined the editorial board of *Ballet Annual* at the same time; we were both founder members of the Gautier Club, an exclusive din-ing club of writers on ballet, who met about twice a year, always with a distinguished guest; and when Mary succeeded to the edito-rial chair of the *Dancing Times* after the sudden death of Arthur Franks in 1963, I was honored to accept her invitation to become editorial adviser to the magazine. *The Dancer's Heritage* has been revised several times since it was first written, and not only have I continued to seek her advice but, most appropriately, the *Dancing Times* has now become its publisher.

In my desire to strike a balance when treating of ballet activities in different parts of the world, I sought the assistance of two dance historians, one from America and the other from France. The first of these was, of course, Lillian Moore, with whom I was then in almost weekly correspondence, although at that time we had met only on the all too rare occasions when she visited Europe. The other was Marie-Françoise Christout, the French historian whose chosen specialty is the Court Ballet, but who is also a critic of considerable experience. Her advice, therefore, was particularly helpful in connection with the early chapters and for the later section on contemporary French ballet.

Another expert eye that scanned my typescript was that of my friend, G. B. L. Wilson, who has photographed thousands of young dancers—his photographic archive, covering a period of several decades now, must be unique—and for more than twenty-one years has written the most informative and entertaining gossip column in the ballet press, "Off Stage," for the *Dancing Times*. We have known one another for more than thirty years, and he does not seem a day older than when we were first introduced by Swin. His jobs—first as manager of a gas works, then as an assistant keeper at the Science Museum—have allowed him time to follow the fortunes of the dance world and to record its *petite histoire* in his entertaining monthly page in the *Dancing Times*, "Off Stage!" Now that he has retired he seems to be more active than ever, and performs a much appreciated service advising young English dancers on employment in foreign companies. A good many years ago now he brought out the first edition of his *Dictionary of Ballet*, which, although other works of the same kind have been published, has maintained its supremacy as an encyclopedia, and as edition has followed edition, I have been happy to supply him with such historical information as he has needed, while he on his side has been one of my "first readers," the other being my wife.

The Dancer's Heritage was one of the first books of mine that he read in draft, and since then he has struggled with a succession of manuscripts, battling without complaint through a maze of deletions, additions, corrections and corrections of corrections. To have one's work scrutinized at this stage by another eye and mind is indispensable, for an author is usually too involved to pick up all the inconsistencies and errors that creep in during writing, and to see where a section needs reworking, how a passage can be rephrased to make its meaning clearer or to give it an easier flow for the reader.

With the benefit of all this attention, *The Dancer's Heritage* took its final shape. I dedicated it to Dame Adeline Genée, and her successor as President of the R.A.D., Dame Margot Fonteyn, did me the honor of writing a foreword. At the time it never occurred to me how much of Margot's precious time I was bespeaking with my request, but over the next few months I realized she, like Genée, was a complete perfectionist. For some weeks after she had agreed to write a foreword there was no word from her. I began to be anxious, and adopted the tactic of appearing in her dressing-room after a performance as a living reminder of her promise. In May 1960, when the book was already at the printers, I received from her what she described as "a very rough draft." It really would have served, but she asked for it to be returned because, as she put it, it was "completely muddle-headed" and she wanted "to bash at it again." Early in July, when I was becoming desperate, a new version, very much better than the first, reached me. I sent it to Blacks at once, for time was now very short. It was to be made more perfect when she corrected the proof, and then came the final flourish of perfectionism when she sent me a cable from Monte Carlo reading: "Please change they in last sentence to we, Regards, Margot."

The success of *The Dancer's Heritage* exceeded my expectations. The first edition, published by Blacks in 1960, was followed two years later by a Penguin edition—a rare accolade. Fortuitously it had come out at the moment when dance history was about to take root, in a modest way, in English schools. In 1967, on the initiative of the R.A.D., ballet was accepted as a subject for the General Certificate of Education (O Level),* and *The Dancer's Heritage* found its place as the standard textbook, a place it has retained ever since. The book, which is now published by the *Dancing Times*, has never been out of print and is now selling faster than ever in its fifth edition.

---

*One of the two examinations for the General Certificate of Education in English secondary education, 'O' denoting Ordinary level as distinguished from 'A' for Advanced level.

CHAPTER FIVE

Bringing the Past to Life

A DANCE historian should not work in isolation from the living theatre. While most of his time has to be spent in libraries and at his
desk, it is vitally important that he should know dancers and understand how theatres and ballet companies operate in the contemporary world. A direct knowledge of what goes on in the theatre, from
decisions made in the director's office to the sweat and toil of rehearsals and the tensions of performance, give the historian a sympathy with his subject, for the basic attitudes of artists and adminis-
trators change little in the course of time. There are also other ways
of bringing the past to life than through the medium of prose, and
the historian may sometimes be called upon to play a positive part in
the re-creation of a ballet from an earlier period. My first experience
in this direction was concerned with one of the greatest master-
pieces in the Royal Ballet repertory, Frederick Ashton's version of
La Fille mal gardée, a ballet with a long and fascinating history
stretching back to the first production by Dauberval on the eve of
the French Revolution.

During the 1950s this ballet lay somewhat outside the confines of
my specialized study, but there was an occasion when I was tempted

to search for the original score which, if it existed, must, I surmised, be in Bordeaux, where the ballet had been created. At first my quest seemed all too easy. The Municipal Librarian of Bordeaux, to whom I wrote, confirmed there was a score which he would send to the Paris Opéra where I could consult it. But my hopes of making an exciting discovery were quickly dashed when the score turned out to be of Duni's opera of the same name.

That was some years before Frederick Ashton asked if I could tell him anything useful about the ballet. He came to dinner with me one evening in Bickley, and we went through my notes, which dealt mainly with the 1828 revival at the Paris Opéra for which Herold had written a new score. Ashton was very concerned about the music, for he only knew the later score by Hertel (written for the Berlin revival of 1864), and this he had rejected as being too heavy in flavor. I drew his attention to Herold's music, which at that time I believed to be the earliest in existence, and arranged for the manuscript full score at the Opéra to be copied. It turned out to be the answer to Ashton's quandary; both he and John Lanchbery, the principal conductor of the Royal Ballet, who had been entrusted with the task of arranging the music, were delighted with it.

My own interest in *La Fille mal gardée* was stimulated too, and becoming curious to know whether Herold had incorporated in his score any of the themes from Duni's opera, I decided to have another look at the score that belonged to the Bordeaux Library. Having acquired a microfilm reader, I ordered a microfilm so as to study it at my leisure. When the film arrived I was staggered by its bulk . . . and by the size of the bill that accompanied it! As I began to view it I realized the Library had just microfilmed all the orchestral parts of the Duni score, and I was beginning to curse myself for lack of forethought in not asking for the first violin part alone when it dawned on me that I had made a great discovery. For, interspersed, higgledy-piggledy, with the opera parts were the parts for the ballet, clearly the score which Dauberval himself had used, in manuscript, bearing many cuts and additions made over the years, and here and there little drawings, one of them obscene, which the musicians had scribbled in their idle moments.

Jack Lanchbery's work in preparing the music was already well advanced when the original score thus came to light, but there was just time for him to use a few passages from it. When he and Ashton had first heard the Herold score they were surprised and disappointed at the absence of any music suitable for a *grand pas de deux,* and my assistance was again invoked. As a result, the Librarian of the Opéra, André Ménetrat, discovered among the orchestral parts for the 1828 production, the music for a *pas de deux* that had been interpolated for Fanny Elssler and her sister in 1837. This turned out to be exactly what was needed, and when I heard Jack play it through one evening at Ashton's house, I was surprised to recognize that most of the melodies used in it came from Donizetti's opera, *L'Elisir d'Amore,* which in 1837 had not been heard in Paris and would therefore have sounded completely fresh. As time went by, Jack and I discovered more and more borrowings in the Herold score: a theme used by Haydn in his 85th symphony, the overture from an opera by Martini, and several passages by Rossini—some descriptive music from the *Barber of Seville,* the storm from *Cenerentola,* and (identified by G. B. L. Wilson) an aria from a little-known opera about Queen Elizabeth which Ashton used for Lise's mime scene. This threw a fascinating light on the practice of composing music for ballet in pre-Romantic times, and Jack Lanchbery and I were inspired to collaborate in a series of articles dealing with the original Bordeaux score, the Herold score and the Royal Ballet score.

By now I was wholly involved, and I put aside my work on the French Romantic ballet to discover as much as I could about *La Fille mal gardée.* I began by investigating the incident which was said to have inspired Dauberval. Beaumont, in giving the anecdote of how the choreographer had seen a print in a shop window while urinating against the wall, had suggested that this might have been a certain engraving by P. A. Baudouin, but that print did not to my mind fit the description. A search through *catalogues raisonnées* led me to another engraving by the same artist, and when I ran it to ground at the Bibliothèque Nationale in Paris (the British Museum did not have a copy), there was no doubt that this was what met Dauberval's eye.

It was evident that the history of this ballet was still waiting to be told, and Arthur Franks, then editor of the *Dancing Times,* agreed to publish a collection of essays on the ballet which I would edit. In a long historical survey, which formed more than a third of the whole collection, I recorded the history of this ballet in detail for the first time. From a manuscript chronicle of theatrical performances in Bordeaux I was able to correct the erroneous date of 1786 for the first performance that until then had slavishly been copied from one book to another. I allowed the Soviet ballet historian, Yuri Slonimsky, with whom I had struck up a friendship by correspondence, to read my essay in typescript, and was glad he was able to make use of my discoveries in his own booklet on the ballet which was published in Russia the following year.

There was an interesting sequel to my participation in this production. In the summer of 1960 Jack Lanchbery and I spent several days at the Paris Opéra going through some old scores which we thought might interest Ashton if he were minded to follow *Fille* with another reconstruction from the past. Jack's ability to play from a full score was to me little short of miraculous. He would glance at it for a moment or two, and then play as if he had rehearsed it for weeks, unerringly picking out the melody, giving it all the expression it demanded, and commenting on it as he went along. We worked through Adam's *Le Corsaire,* which Jack found full of dramatic effect but somewhat carelessly written, Halévy's *Manon Lescaut,* and another old ballet by Dauberval, *Le Page inconstant.*

Manon excited us most of all, for it was composed with great skill and made use of *leitmotiv* more than ten years earlier than *Giselle,* which was previously thought to have broken new ground in this respect. We hoped Ashton would use this score for a full-length ballet, and I even amused myself by reworking the scenario which Scribe had originally written for Aumer. In the end the subject was used by Kenneth MacMillan, who to my regret preferred to use far less satisfactory music by Massenet in preference to the Halévy score, which he may never have examined.

Le Page inconstant was a ballet version of *The Marriage of Figaro,* first produced in Bordeaux shortly before *Fille.* We looked at several scores for this ballet—the original Bordeaux music, and later scores by Gyrowetz and Habeneck. At one moment Jack stopped playing and said to me: "You'll think I'm joking when you hear the next number." He then proceeded to play the apotheosis of *The Sleeping Beauty!* The melody was in fact an old French song called "Vive Henri IV," which had been inserted into the original score and later used by Tchaikovsky. Jack Lanchbery was very taken by *Le Page inconstant,* seeing Margot Fonteyn as Cherubino, but unfortunately nothing came of this either, for Ashton decided, no doubt with a wise instinct, that it was time to turn his attention to more contemporary subjects.

Later I was to be privileged to make an indirect contribution to a number of historical revivals. This came about through a stroke of good fortune—or was it genius on my part?—the secret of which I now willingly divulge so others can follow my example. Guest's Law, as I propounded it, is that a dance historian should marry a dance notator. In 1962 I successfully put this Law to the proof by marrying Ann Hutchinson, who is not only the foremost authority on Labanotation but has studied the notation of movement in such depth that I do not think there is a method of any importance in existence which she cannot read.

Ann had entered my life towards the end of 1955. Earlier that year John Baker of Phoenix House, for whom I was then writing my *Fanny Cerrito*, sent me a copy of an American book for my advice on whether he should publish an English edition. It may not have been exactly in my line, but I boldly did my best. Entitled *Labanotation*, it was a manual of an established system of dance notation which I found surprisingly comprehensible and readable, considering the technical nature of the subject. Before giving my opinion I made a few enquiries and ascertained that Dame Ninette de Valois was planning to introduce this system to record the repertory of the Royal Ballet. This information I duly imparted to John Baker with a recommendation that the book should be published, and the English edition came out in time for the Christmas market and I was invited to a publication party at the English Speaking Union to meet the authoress.

I went along expecting to be presented to a forbidding scholar, no doubt with thick glasses, hair drawn back tightly into an austere bun, and a strident voice, and instead was introduced to a very attractive blonde with a gentle manner and enchanting dimples. Some days later we met again at a reception where there was opportunity to talk. I asked her the conventional question of whether she was on her first visit to England, and was told, "No, I was educated here . . . at a school in Littlehampton." Ann has told me since that she had never before added the precise location of the school, but on this occasion it certainly produced a startling effect. "Good heavens," I cried, "but I was at school in Littlehampton too!" and we found we had spent several years of our childhood only a block apart from one another, and we even remembered a visit by the girls of her school to see my school's revue, for which I was in charge of the lights. Afterwards there was a dance which, in my recollection, was a rather ignominious experience for a schoolboy whose main interest lay in the cricketing feats of Don Bradman. Ann remembers the evening too, but for another reason—for having danced with a boy "with two left feet," as she puts it, who may well have been me!

After leaving her school at Littlehampton, Ann, having expressed a wish to be a dancer, was sent to Dartington Hall, which had been chosen by her parents not because of the method of dance taught there but because of its pleasant situation in the Devon countryside. It was there, at the Jooss-Leeder School, that she was introduced to what was then called "Tanzschrift," the system of recording movement originally invented by Rudolf Laban. She became so proficient at it that Kurt Jooss commissioned her, when she was still a student, to notate his famous ballet *The Green Table*. Then the war broke out, and in 1940 Ann, being an American citizen, went to New York, where she lived for the next twenty-one years. In order to be accepted for professional engagements, she began extending her dance experience by studying ballet (both Russian and Cecchetti methods) and some of the modern dance techniques including, notably, those of Martha Graham and Humphrey-Weidman. This gave her the basic accomplishments she needed for the Broadway theatre, where she danced in a series of successful musicals under some of America's leading choreographers, Jerome Robbins, Agnes de Mille, Michael Kidd, Hanya Holm. It also expanded her understanding of movement and gave her an exceptional background for what, from the very beginning, was her main interest—dance notation. Within a few months of arriving in New York she and three other enthusiasts, with the encouragement of the critic John Martin, founded the Dance Notation Bureau, which thanks to her vision and perseverance grew into the firmly established organization that she was eventually able to hand over to her successors. Over these years, and since, she made a most significant contribution towards the development of Laban's original idea from the relatively primitive state in which he left it to the highly sophisticated and flexible system it is today. It was she who coined the name under which it is most widely known—Labanotation.

When our friendship began she was in Europe on a Rockefeller grant and hoping to see Labanotation accepted by the Royal Ballet. Unfortunately, not only for Ann but also for the dance, which still has to achieve proper recognition as a subject suitable for serious academic study, Ninette de Valois changed her mind and decided, so to speak, to "buy British" in the form of a less scientific and less precise system that had just been invented by Rudolf Benesh, the husband of one of her dancers. A great opportunity was thus lost, but that story belongs more properly to Ann's memoirs than to mine. For the next year and a half, when Ann was still on this side of the Atlantic, our friendship developed in a platonic way, and after her return to America we kept in touch by correspondence, our letters, as we noticed later when re-reading them, becoming noticeably warmer in tone as time went on. Some years later, in 1961, she revisited England for a notation conference, and we discovered, quite suddenly, that we had fallen in love.

We were married the following January and have been living happily ever after in Holland Park, one of London's most pleasant districts, surrounded by a growing accumulation of books and papers.

As an historian I could not help but be stirred by the idea of the many dances that had been recorded long ago in old notation systems, waiting for just such a person as Ann. Let me make it clear, however, that she and I were not the first to be aware of this treasure of ancient choreography. A number of specialists in historical dance had studied the Feuillet notation system in considerable depth, but for one reason or another they had made little mark on the wide world of the dance except—regrettably—to exasperate others by an apparent inability to present a united front of mutual respect. This has done much harm to an excellent cause, and is in sad contrast with the spirit of cooperation that exists among theatre historians who specialize in ballet. But I digress. Having gained some knowledge of the notated materials extant, I gave Ann a series of cunningly selected presents which, over the years, have produced practical demonstrations of what these notations can reveal if they are effectively deciphered.

One such gift was the English edition of F. A. Zorn's *Grammar of the Art of Dancing,* in which he gave as an example the *Cachucha* which Fanny Elssler made so famous. At that time, in the late 1960s, I was writing a biography of Elssler, so I had a special interest in seeing it revived. One evening at a party I broached the idea to Peter Brinson, who was then directing Ballet for All, the Royal Ballet's educational group. His response was immediate and enthusiastic, and it was soon decided that Ann would revive it as a highlight in the program, "The World of Giselle." Ann took Zorn's book with her on our holiday to Crete in the summer of 1967, and worked out the dance in a quiet corner of the grounds of the Palace of Minos at Knossos. On our return home, she enlisted the help of her assistant, Philippa Heale, who had made a profound study of Spanish dancing, and together they ironed out a number of details that were unclear, and produced a definitive score in Labanotation. Meanwhile the Royal Opera House's costume department brilliantly reconstructed the costume from the evidence of old prints and the measurements I made of Elssler's costume in Vienna, and Jack Lanchbery arranged the music for two guitars, piano and castanets. The dance remained in the Ballet for All repertory for several years, but when Brinson left, the respect for authenticity, which was the hallmark of his direction, disappeared and the authentic version was replaced by an "interpretation" of the dance by Kenneth MacMillan. I did not see this, but it seemed to show a regrettable unawareness of tradition in an enterprise that presumably purported to have an educational purpose.

The *Cachucha* was also produced in Vienna during the centenary season of the State Opera House. Christl Zimmerl, the leading Austrian ballerina, came to London specially to learn it from Ann, and it was one of the highlights of the celebrations. Sadly, Christl died a few years later, and it was recorded in her obituary in *The Times* that one of her greatest satisfactions had been to bring back Fanny Elssler's *Cachucha* to Vienna. Among the English dancers who have performed it, by far the best interpretation has been that of Margaret Barbieri, who danced it at the R.A.D. Assembly in 1972 and showed that, relatively simple though it seems to be, it requires the experience and sensitivity of a mature ballerina to bring out its inner subtleties, as Fanny Elssler, the most expressive dancer of her day, had done. Later, in 1980, we were able to make a film record of her performance in this historic dance.

Another of my presents to Ann was Saint-Léon's manual of his notation method, *La Sténochorégraphie,* a method that was remarkably precise for its time, although designed specifically for classical ballet. Saint-Léon was an exceptional virtuoso in an age when male dancers were generally eclipsed by the ballerinas. He was also celebrated as a choreographer, and one of the special points of interest in his book is the example he gives of his notation method—the complete choreographic score of the *pas de six* from *La Vivandière,* a set-piece for himself and his wife Fanny Cerrito, and four supporting *danseuses.* As I had intended, this too came under Ann's scrutiny, for Saint-Léon's symbols held no secrets from her. She transcribed it during a holiday in Spain, and then tried it out on her pupils at the R.A.D. Teachers' Training Course. Aside from its historical value as perhaps the most authentic example of choreography from the Romantic period—uncorrupted by any failings of human memory—it proved to be a delightful work on its own account, and early in 1976 Ann was asked by Robert Joffrey to mount it for his second company. In the outcome it made such an impression on Joffrey that it was presented, in 1977, by the senior company of the Joffrey Ballet, receiving unanimous acclaim from the critics.

In terms of working hours the part I played in these revivals was secondary, but their realization was due in the first place to the initiative I provided in my role of historian. Another enterprise with which I was concerned was Ballet for All's revival of extracts from the traditional version of *Coppélia*. This derived directly from Saint-Léon's original production of 1870, which to my great distress had been dropped from the repertory of the Opéra early in the 1960s in favor of a brash new production. Peter Brinson was interested in presenting a program on the history of *Coppélia* for Ballet for All, based on my historical research, and on my recommendation Paulette Dynalix came to London to produce extracts from the traditional French version with the role of Frantz played in travesty by a woman. Paulette, who had played the part with memorable sensitivity, stayed with us several times when she was mounting this work, and our flat sparkled with her wit. In 1970, the centenary year of the ballet, the production was expanded for a slightly larger group and virtually the whole of the first two acts was revived. The only significant cuts, inevitable in view of the dancers available, were the large ensembles. Ann played an important part in this venture by recording it all in Labanotation, and one day we took a film of Paulette performing all the mime scenes. At the time it seemed we were salvaging a choreographic gem which would have otherwise slipped into oblivion, but happily there has been a change of heart at the Paris Opéra, where Pierre Lacotte has recently restored the traditional version.

Monsieur Pierre Joseph Victor de Besenval Baron de Bronnstatt
au Croix de l'Ordre Royal et Militaire de St. Louis,   Lieutenant général des Armées du Roy, Inspecteur
général des Regimens Suisses et Grisons,   Gouverneur de la Ville d'Haguenau en Alsace
Lieutenant Colonel du Regiment des Gardes Suisses.

The print that gave Dauberval the inspiration for *La Fille mal gardée.*

Left: Ann Hutchinson working out Fanny Elssler's *Cachucha* in the Palace of Minos, Knossos in 1967.

Below: Margaret Barbieri and Janet Francis in the Ballet for All reconstruction of *Coppélia,* wearing costumes based on the original 1870 designs.

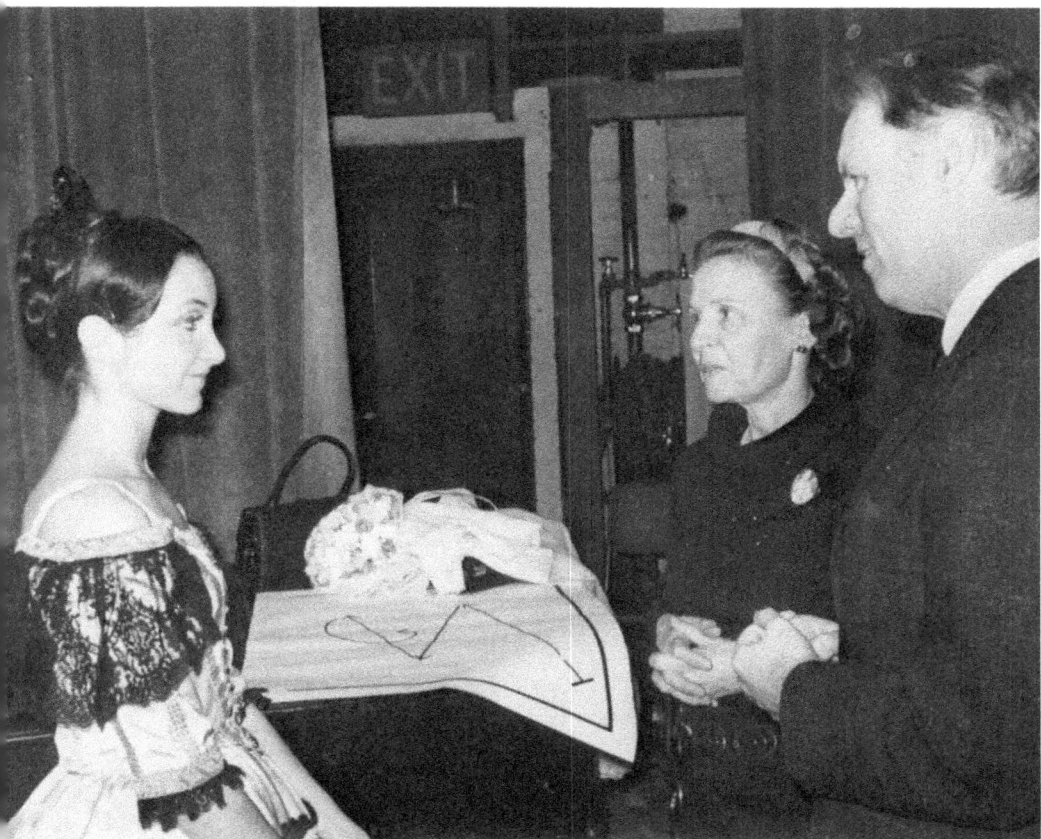

Margaret Barbieri, in the *Cachucha* costume, with Ivor and Ann Guest at the Royal Academy of Dancing Assembly in 1972. Photo: G.B.L. Wilson.

Above: Margot Fonteyn with Ann and Ivor Guest at the Royal Academy of Dancing, 1969. Photo: G.B.L. Wilson.

Below: Ivor Guest with John Saunders and Alan Hooper, Administrative and Artistic Directors of the R.A.D., Summer, 1980. Photo: Jennie Walton.

Ivor Guest with Princess Margaret at the opening of the "Spotlight" exhibition, organized by the Theatre Museum and opened on April 7, 1981.

Above: Ivor Guest, as Chairman of the R.A.D., showing the Queen the Adeline Genée exhibition at the new headquarters building in 1974.

Right: Fanny Elssler's *Cachucha* costume, preserved in Vienna.

Above: Ivor Guest with Carlotta Zambelli, 1960. Photo: Max Erlanger de Rosen.

Right: Ivor Guest and Edwin Binney 3rd at the Romantic Ballet exhibition mounted by Harvard Theatre Collection in 1966, commemorating their books. Photo: Carolyn Jakeman.

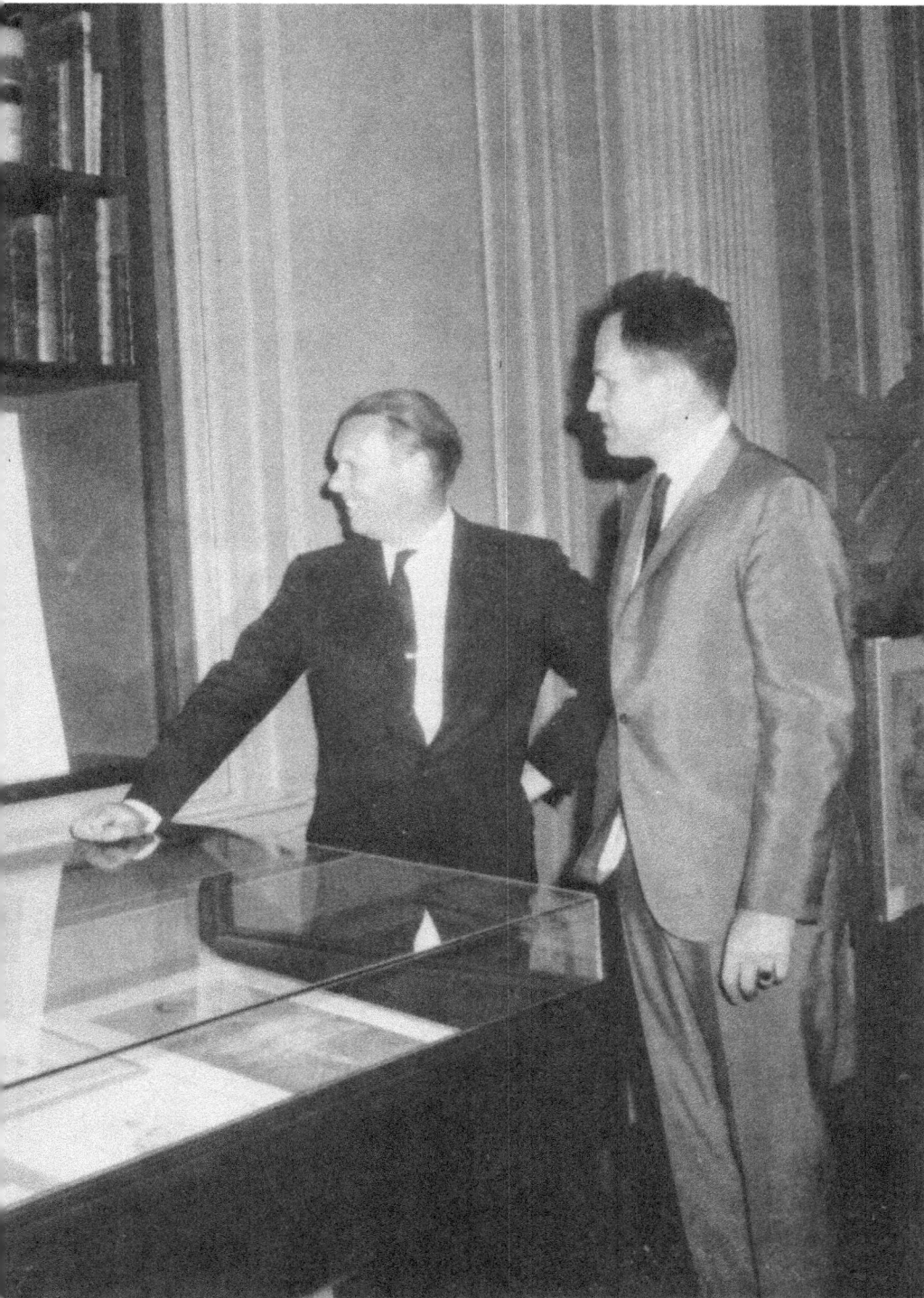

Page from the manuscript of *The Divine Virginia* (New York and Basle, 1977).

daughter's protector.

hopefully

~~Meanwhile, there~~ Virginia ~~was forced to~~

abandon ~~for a while~~ ~~continued to~~

~~daily class~~ ~~a few~~

~~infidelity~~

~~to him~~

an engagement in Messina. After a *few weeks he could bear*
his ~~together~~ no longer and ~~turned~~ up in Messina. His
~~presence did not pass unnoticed, and~~

One evening when he was in the theatre, a section of the
~~audience~~ hissed Virginia on her entrance. *He felt this as*
a personal ~~affront~~.
~~Turning~~ to General della Rocca, who was
with him, *he heatedly exclaimed*: "The fools think they are
hissing *my* dancer. Tomorrow she will be my wife."
~~His mother~~, *however*, had more ambitious plans for
him. He was recalled to Turin, and shortly afterwards
Virginia received an offer of 50,000 francs *for the*
~~return~~ *of* his letters. She refused, and when the price was
raised, returned the same answer. "I will return
these souvenirs of our love," she wrote to him, "if you
ask for them yourself. *Surely it is not* ~~you~~ who have allowed me
to be insulted?" The Count assured her that he had
had no part in this. He left her with the letters,

*had misled a ~~I~~ jump and fallen into the
prompter's box. Emmanuel Alfred ~~wanted~~
~~to~~ ~~reconcile~~ ~~renounce~~ ~~his~~ ~~hatred~~ ~~and had~~
~~their~~ life together was unworthy, she may have done
so. But ~~she~~ ~~her~~ ~~~~ ~~~~ ~~~~ ~~~~ ~~~~ ~~~~ ~~~~
his ungratefulness to he to leave him and*

*Virginia claimed that she gave up her career for some
years, but this was ~~~~.
~~through~~ the end of 1870 she was dancing at the Teatro
~~~~ Regola in Florence, where she gained an
unexpected triumph in ~~~~, taking over the
title role at short notice after Carolina Pochini*

Left: Arthur Saint-Léon.

Below: Virginia Zucchi and her daughter Marie. A family snapshot of the great dancer in her retirement.

"The woman my husband is in love with." Virginia Zucchi in 1873, aged twenty-four.

CHAPTER SIX

The R.A.D. and the Theatre Museum

LEST it be thought that I escaped into flights of historical fancy whenever I took off my lawyer's hat, it is necessary to digress from my literary labors to tell of my involvement with two bodies that have taken up much of my time and energy—the Royal Academy of Dancing and the Theatre Museum.

When I accepted the chairmanship of the Academy in 1969, Peter Brinson, who at that time had a much more intimate knowledge of it than I did, told me bluntly that I was making a mistake and that I should not let myself be distracted from my main task of writing ballet history. There have been times, I must admit, when I have thought how right he was, but in looking back now I have no regrets at having accepted the challenge of restoring the fortunes and standing of the Academy.

I had become aware of the Academy's existence when writing my biography of Genée. She was the most distinguished and the most influential of its founders, and after her retirement as a dancer she had served as Chairman and President for thirty-four years and seen it grow into a worldwide organization with a royal charter. The last chapter of my book on her was almost entirely concerned with the

Academy, and the research for it brought me in touch with Kathleen Gordon, the Academy's Director, who had joined it in 1924 and knew more about its inner workings than anyone else. Miss Gordon gave me several evenings of her time to reminisce about Genée, and I soon found myself repaying her kindness by joining the committee of the R.A.D. Production Club and writing an occasional book review for the R.A.D. Gazette.

In 1965 Sir Ashley Clarke, who had recently become Chairman, invited me to join the Executive Committee, I felt extremely honored, but I was reluctant to accept a commitment that might demand more time than I could afford, for I was then heavily embroiled in the activities of London Dance Theatre. But I was assured there would be few obligations beyond attending quarterly meetings, and in fact for the first few years I played a very small role in the Academy's affairs.

My first contribution of any substance was concerned with the proposal, initiated by the Academy, to introduce ballet as a subject for the General Certificate of Education (O Level). Sitting on the working party which steered this project to its successful conclusion, I was amazed at the skill of the educationalists among our number in handling the government committees on whose approval all depended. My own task, in collaboration with Keith Lester, was to advise on the form of the examination and to produce specimen examination questions. When the examination was introduced Keith and I became responsible, for several years, for writing the questions for the ballet history papers.

An unusual feature of this examination was the "Project File" which the candidate had to compile on a subject of his own choice having some bearing on ballet. For some years, in default of anyone else, I marked these files, a chore that demanded several days' concentrated work but produced, as compensation, the occasional moment of hilarity. A few of the files were refreshingly original, but others were quite shamefacedly copied, without acknowledgment, from books. I found it an intriguing exercise to detect plagiarisms of this sort, and more than once I recognized my own work! Sometimes, of course, a candidate would give herself away, such as the fourteen-year-old who unthinkingly incorporated the phrase, "As Benois once said to me . . . ." There were other welcome moments of light relief. I remember in particular a project on Martha Graham in which a candidate with an unusually vivid imagination wrote of one of her ballets as being inspired by "the 1929 stock market crash in which thousands of American youths were lost." Then, some of the projects were the product of true enthusiasm, if at times over-expressed. To cite an example, Tchaikovsky surely never had a more passionate admirer than the girl who ended her essay with the following passage: "Perhaps the composer wrote these brilliant scores to save everyone from becoming like lifeless zombies or dull, uninteresting, identical dummies, which I am quite sure would have happened to the human race if God had not been so pitiful and realized that the world needed a great composer of music to bring light and life back into the hearts of the people of such a cruel world." Whew!

At the meetings of the Academy's Executive Committee, however, the achievement of establishing an O Level examination in ballet was completely overshadowed by the pressing need to find new premises. At the time of my election the Academy was situated, very conveniently for me, in two houses in Holland Park. From one of these the worldwide examinations based on the Academy's ballet syllabi were administered, while the other housed the Teachers' Training Course ("the T.T.C.")—literally, for at that time the students were boarded on the premises. This latter property was unfortunately held on a lease whose term had only a few years to run, and to complicate matters the freehold had just been purchased over the Academy's head. This predicament was seen by the Chairman as a challenge, and at one of my first committee meetings we were shown a beautifully constructed architect's model of a floor in a new building in the Barbican district of the City of London. It looked very impressive, but I found it difficult to see how the Academy, with its limited resources, could possibly afford the cost of conversion and the rent.

This project was abandoned, but time was running out fast when we first heard about South Lodge, a large mansion standing in its own ground on the south side of Knightsbridge, almost opposite the Guards barracks. The prospect of the Academy being established in surroundings that were at once so accessible and prestigious was hard to resist and most of us were stirred, perhaps more than we should have been, by the vision it offered for the future. Terms were agreed for the purchase, and we were assured that the bank would make finance available for the very extensive conversion that was planned and that this borrowing would be reduced, if not altogether cleared, by money raised by public appeal. It seemed to be viable, and only a few voices counseled caution at the euphoric General Meeting that approved the purchase.

Alas, matters then began to go awry. The appeal was a failure, the extent of which was demonstrated by the arrival of a cheque for a derisory £10 from Paul Getty, the oil magnate—a piece of paper which someone suggested the Academy should frame, uncashed, for its curiosity value! Much more serious, however, were the effects of the economic crisis that took everyone by surprise, shaking the country out of the apparent prosperity of the sixties and bringing in its train severe restrictions on borrowing and soaring interest rates. In these circumstances the Academy found it had overstretched itself and was on the brink of insolvency. My first inkling of the seriousness of the situation came after a meeting of a subcommittee considering the revision of the Royal Charter, when I heard two of the other members speaking in hushed tones of the possibility of insolvency. Building work on the conversion was halted, and everyone was plunged into despair.

This rapidly mounting crisis coincided with a change of Director, for the experienced Kathleen Gordon, who had been at the helm for as long as many of us could remember, had resigned in 1968. It should be recorded that she was one of the few who considered it folly to embark so soon on the conversion of South Lodge, although that was not the main reason for her resignation. When the Executive Committee first considered the question of her successor, Phyllis Bedells proposed my name. I was very touched, but had to explain that I could not abandon my legal practice. The choice eventually rested on Peter Brinson who, straining to wield a new broom, presented an imaginative and far-reaching paper on the reorganization of the Academy, which was accepted by the members at the Annual General Meeting in January 1969. But almost immediately these brave plans for the future turned horribly sour with the realization that the Academy was in danger of collapse.

It was a traumatic year that I would not wish to live through again. Brinson resigned, complaining bitterly that he had not been fully informed of the Academy's plight, and on my advice the Executive Committee was hastily summoned to consider the situation with the auditors. It fell to me to ask the painful question whether the Academy might be insolvent, and I received the answer that this could well be so if South Lodge was worth no more than the Academy's property expert advised. I then said bluntly that the Academy had no choice but to sell South Lodge, for it was being strangled by the interest charges on the enormous loan taken out to help pay for the purchase and the conversion. In the event the Academy was to be saved at the eleventh hour by obtaining a price for South Lodge far beyond what we had been advised was its value, but the confidence of the members had been shattered by the risks that had been taken, and the Chairman and the Finance Committee tendered their resignations when the decision to sell was confirmed by the members at an Extraordinary General Meeting.

All this was a personal tragedy for Sir Ashley Clarke, who had toiled for the Academy without thought for his health and was left to shoulder the responsibility for the near-disaster. Risks had been taken which events showed to be imprudent, but if his boldness had paid off, as it might have done had circumstances been propitious, he would no doubt have been hailed for his imaginative leadership. Such is the way of life!

Ashley then wrote to ask me to take the chair at the next Executive Committee meeting, fixed for November 11th, and recognizing the implication of his request, I felt obliged to reply plainly that I doubted whether I would have the time to undertake so onerous a task. Right up to the last moment I was of two minds whether to attend that meeting, but in the end a voice inside told me I could not shirk my duty and so, on that fateful day, I faced the worried remnant of the Executive Committee, whose devotion and dedication were to set the Academy on course again and bring it safely out of the stormy seas in which it had so nearly foundered. I felt it right to explain what were my other commitments, and I accepted the chairmanship on a strictly provisional basis, in the expectation that someone more suitable would shortly be found.

The problems before us seemed so formidable in those early days that there were times when I wished myself free of the responsibilities I had allowed myself to assume. I even dreaded the arrival of the post lest it brought news of some unforeseen problem to complicate my existence still further. There were untidy threads from the South Lodge venture to be unraveled, and the most pressing problem, that of finding new premises, loomed over us like an awesome juggernaut. The sale of South Lodge, which was due to be completed in a few weeks time, would leave the Academy without a roof over its head and with a surplus that was very modest in relation to its requirements. The second problem was to find a Director, for Peter Brinson had not been replaced and the very efficient Administrative Director, Marjorie Kimberley, had decided to join a leading firm of accountants. Thirdly, the Executive Committee had been reduced to the barest minimum by the resignations, and needed to be strengthened particularly by the injection of expertise in the business field.

I had to face my first hurdle at the Annual General Meeting in

January 1970. With Dame Margot Fonteyn, the Academy's President, at my side, it was my task to present the Executive Committee's report and the accounts to a gathering of teachers who were still deeply disturbed by the way their Academy was being managed. To me there seemed nothing amusing about that meeting at the time, but to an uninvolved spectator it must have had a surrealist quality, as G. B. L. Wilson described in his report for the *Dancing Times*. His account caused the sort of offense people in wartime feel when fun is made of their patriotism, but though at the time I thought it lacking in taste, I can now appreciate it as a brilliant and accurate piece of comic writing. The meeting began to get out of hand almost as soon as it began, when it was discovered there were people present who were not members of the Academy, and among those who got up to leave was Madame Idzikowski, who as the wife of the great Stanislas Idzikowski had always been welcome in the past. It was all very embarrassing, and the uproar was only quelled when Dame Ninette de Valois restored our equanimity by suggesting that this was perhaps the moment for someone to recite "The Charge of the Light Brigade." Another member then rose and said, very seriously, "No, we should have a few minutes' prayer." As G. B. L. Wilson put it, "This rather stunned the members— suppose God were a member of the Cecchetti Society?"

After all this, the business of the meeting got under way, but the going was very hard. For a time I was afraid no one would propose the adoption of the report and accounts, but eventually, after some patient cajoling, a proposer and seconder were found and the resolution was put to the vote and carried, although most of the members glumly abstained. It took two hours to reach the end of the agenda, and when we moved on to the cocktail party we found many of our guests had given us up in despair and gone home. G. B. L. Wilson described me as "unflappable" on that occasion, but I certainly did not feel unperturbed!

I would not care to go through that experience again. I felt very isolated at that cocktail party, for very few members then knew me. But happily the tide turned and a year later, at the next Annual General Meeting, a very healthy set of accounts was presented and it was clear the members' confidence had been restored in good measure. In the intervening twelve months the Academy had had a stroke of good fortune for which no one would have dared to hope. After the sale of South Lodge had been completed, the Academy was allowed to remain in occupation rent-free, while the purchasers were sorting out their planning problems. As a result of this privilege, which was granted as a personal favor to Margot Fonteyn, the Academy remained in the decaying building for two and a half years and we were able to restore its finances to a strength far exceeding the most optimistic expectations.

The departure of Marjorie Kimberley left the Academy without an administrative head, and I persuaded Iris Truscott, who had joined the Executive Committee at about the same time as myself, to hold the fort while we sought a General Secretary. This she did with great skill and without remuneration, gaining an experience of the inner working of the Academy that has proved to be of inestimable value to the Committee. A conscious decision was made to retain the artistic control of the Academy in the hands of the Executive Committee, and to seek someone from the business world to take charge of the administration. To fill the post we engaged a former executive of Rootes, Barrie Dumont, who was given the brief of continuing the economies which had been decreed by the Executive Committee.

For some months I was expecting to be relieved of the responsibilities of the chairmanship, but in the Spring, on my fiftieth birthday to be precise, I was elected unanimously as permanent Chairman. By that time I had formed definite views on the constitution of the Executive Committee. For it to be really effective, the distinguished dance teaching element, which had been strengthened by the addition of Dame Ninette de Valois who gave great support to the Academy in its darkest hour, needed to be complemented by men and women who would bring professional expertise in a number of fields that bore on the Academy's activities and, what was specially important, would be prepared to give generously of their time. A seat on a royal institution is an enviable status symbol, but I wanted no one who was not prepared to make a real contribution. I also wanted to spread the non-dance element as broadly as possible, and the result, as I write, is that we have representatives from the fields of education, law, accountancy, the stock exchange, business management, banking and public relations who, together with a number of dedicated dance teachers, make up a truly balanced and widely competent executive body.

In 1972 the Academy was given notice that it would have to vacate South Lodge in the summer, and its efforts to find a permanent headquarters were redoubled. For a time it seemed that a double move would be inevitable, and the Academy was on the point of committing itself to a short lease of a former department store in Seven Sisters Road as a temporary home while more suitable quarters were sought, when a member of the Academy staff, driving to work, noticed a "To Let" board outside a large warehouse in Battersea. I convened an Executive Committee meeting at the shortest possible notice, and as we walked through the empty building the imaginations of all of us were fired by what it promised. It seemed the answer to our prayers, and so it was. There was all the space we could see the Academy needing, wooden floors were already laid throughout that, with a little sanding, would be ideal for dance studios, and on the first floor was a vast, well-lit room we envisaged at once as the principal studio. Events moved extraordinarily fast. The decision to take the premises was made in April, the architects produced plans for the conversion, the lawyers settled the terms of the twenty-year lease, and within a few weeks the builders moved in to carry out preliminary works so that the administrative staff could move in at the end of July and the Teachers' Training Course could take possession of the top floor at the beginning of the term in September. This complicated operation was organized with great efficiency by Philip Starr, who had succeeded Barrie Dumont at the beginning of the year.

For more than a year administrative staff, examiners, and the eighty-odd girls of the T.T.C. and their teachers shared the premises with the builders. To reach their studios on the third floor the T.T.C. students had to climb a staircase erected on scaffolding outside the building, and were issued track suits to keep them warm . . . and also to hold in check the carnal instincts of the builders! The builders' task was, of course, greatly complicated by this mixed occupation, which added considerably to the expense of the conversion, but was offset by saving the cost of hiring temporary studios for the T.T.C. (even assuming that such accommodation could have been found) and it was an added advantage to have the General Secretary on the site to cope with the day-to-day problems that inevitably arise in such a complicated building operation. This was a time of rising inflation, and it was not surprising that the original estimates were greatly exceeded. The Executive Committee, who had been deeply affected by the South Lodge crisis, was exceptionally sensitive to these escalating costs, but when the conversion was finished and all the bills were settled, the Academy had managed to pay for it without borrowing a penny and was still left with a healthy reserve. It was a very heartening achievement.

The new headquarters were a source of great pride. The offices were roomy, and there were no less than ten dance studios, changing rooms, a canteen and an impressive entrance hall. In November

1974 all our efforts and anxieties received their reward when the Queen, the Academy's patron, formally opened the building. With Dame Margot I had the privilege of receiving Her Majesty, presenting to her the Vice-Presidents, Committee members, Governors of the T.T.C. and representatives from overseas and the regions of the United Kingdom, escorting her round the building, where various activities had been arranged, and taking tea with her. It was an unforgettable occasion, and even the tea party had an aura of pageantry from the Age of Chivalry. The Queen and her suite were entertained in one of the studios, beneath a colorful tent such as might have adorned some medieval tourney, while the rest of those present looked on, sipping their tea standing up.

In one of the smaller studios was an exhibition devoted to Adeline Genée, and it was my privilege to be Her Majesty's guide, explaining the significance of the various objects. On the last table one of Genée's ballet slippers attracted the attention of the Queen, who asked how long a pair might have lasted. Dame Margot, who was with us, interposed that when she danced a full-length ballet, she wore out three pairs a night, and these last few words filtered through to the corridor where a local reporter was straining his ears to catch a quotation from the royal lips. This was the explanation of the curious headline that appeared on the front page of the following week's issue of the *South London Press:* "Queen sighs: I can wear out six shoes a night."

The financial problems and the move to new premises had not been allowed to interrupt the work of the Academy, which is concerned mainly with the examining of dance students, from the small child to the budding professional, nor to inhibit it from initiating new projects. The increasing demand for the Academy's examinations, both at home and overseas, was met in spite of an ever-present difficulty of training enough examiners of the required caliber. A new Children's Syllabus, devised by Margot Fonteyn, was introduced, followed by the development of an entirely new syllabus for the older child who has passed the children's grades but cannot spare the time needed to prepare for the major examinations. This was the Dance Education Syllabus, worked out by Keith Lester, which imaginatively looked beyond technique to interpretation and a feeling for the style of the Romantic period.

The Teachers' Training Course, which is today known as the College of the Academy, has always been close to my heart. In its early days, before I became Chairman, it had been kept somewhat apart from the other activities, but it is now accepted as an essential and integral part of the Academy. Over the years I have been encouraged to see its curriculum develop under successive Principals—Keith Lester, Patricia Mackenzie, Valerie Taylor, and now Susan Danby—to embrace related subjects that give the ballet teacher an awareness of ballet as an art within the wider family of dance and at the same time enrich his or her intellectual and cultural background by the study of dance history, movement analysis and notation, anatomy and child psychology. It is difficult to cover all these subjects as thoroughly as one would wish, even in a three-year course, but in the past twelve years much progress has been made in this direction without prejudice to the quality of the ballet teaching, which is, after all, the prime purpose of the course. Recently, too, much thought has been given to the possibility of integrating the course into teacher training in the state system, with the object of the Academy's diploma being taken into account towards a teaching qualification, but this development still lies in the future.

Another innovation has been the Professional Dancers' Teaching Course, in which dancers who have retired from a performing career can retrain as teachers. Although the idea for this had already been mooted, the impetus for the course came suddenly, in the summer of 1974, through the Royal Ballet's decision not to renew the contract of Johaar Mosaval, one of its finest character dancers. Mosaval was shattered by his dismissal. He came to see me, and I decided something must be done to help him. Within a few weeks an intensive four-week course had been set up under the direction of Valerie Taylor, and Johaar and five other students enrolled. When the Executive Committee next met, the project was enthusiastically endorsed, and it has since gone from strength to strength. The yearly intake is now about twelve. The length of the course has been extended to nine months, and it has already paid handsome dividends by producing several new examiners for the Academy.

Meanwhile, the need for a more decisive artistic direction had been voiced by a number of Committee members, Dame Margot among them, and after the question had been considered by a small working party, it was decided to appoint an Artistic Director who would function in parallel with the General Administrator. By a fortunate coincidence John Field, who was himself a member of the Executive Committee, had just returned to England after a three-year spell as director of the ballet at La Scala, Milan. He and I used to lunch together occasionally at the Garrick Club, of which we are both members, and one day I asked if he would consider applying for the post himself. To my delight he said he would, and in the summer of 1975 he was unanimously appointed. The hope that he and Philip Starr would be able to establish a satisfactory working relationship was not, however, fulfilled, and after a few months, in April 1976, John Field assumed overall control as Director.

From the outset of my chairmanship I had recognized the importance of a close mutual confidence and understanding existing between the Chairman and the administrative head of the Academy, and although I had striven hard to this end, it was not until John Field's appointment that I felt I had achieved this. No doubt I had expected too much from his predecessors, but what they lacked and what John was able to supply was the professional touch and, specifically, the authority that convinced the Executive Committee that the time had come to abolish the unwieldy Professional Committee and, subject to control in matters of policy, to place the artistic direction firmly in the hands of the Director. He also freed the Academy from the tensions which had strained it so much during its years of peril and recovery, and selected the present Administrative Director, John Saunders, an Australian possessing a happy blend of administrative flair, humanity and humor.

In the summer of 1979 John was offered post of Artistic Director of London Festival Ballet, and left the Academy to return to the professional theatre where his ambitions really lay. We could not hope to replace him with a successor of similar charisma, but with considerable vision the Executive Committee accepted my recommendation that a much younger man, Alan Hooper, be appointed as Artistic Director, working in tandem with John Saunders. These two soon proved themselves an excellent team, bringing to their task a vitality that the Academy had previously lacked.

Almost overnight a new sense of purpose pervaded the Academy. With extraordinary energy Alan initiated an artistic policy that was grounded on his own very considerable experience as a teacher and examiner, and more important, on an understanding of the needs of the teachers who make up the majority of the Academy's membership. At the same time the Academy's international role has been greatly strengthened. Both Alan and John have made exhausting tours around the world, visiting most of the forty-three countries where the Academy is established, and cultivating the ties that link all these centres into one cohesive whole.

The transformation that has taken place over the past two years has been extraordinary, and as I write, in the autumn of 1981, in the twelfth year of my chairmanship, I am deriving real satisfaction from seeing the Academy prosper. I often think of Dame Adeline

Genée, who died, in April 1970, when the Academy's fortunes were still at a low ebb, and hope that she was able to sense the revival that was just beginning and that, from the Dancer's Valhalla, she is now contentedly looking down on her Academy triumphant once again.

*   *   *   *   *   *

The part I played in the events leading up to the establishment of the Theatre Museum is less dramatic. It began with my joining the Society for Theatre Research, on whose committee I served for a number of years. That estimable Society has spawned a number of other organizations, one of which was the British Theatre Museum Association whose object was to stimulate public interest in the formation of a national theatre museum. I was closely involved with this enterprise from the beginning, first as a member of the ad hoc committee that investigated the whole question of theatre museums, and then as an original committee member of the British Theatre Museum Association, whose constitution I drafted. The committee met once a month in the Board Room of Coutts Bank under the successive chairmanships of Laurence Irving, Lord Norwich and Donald Sinden, and for the first few years progress was modest but steady. By 1963 our resources had grown to the point where we felt we could open a small museum in a gallery of Leighton House and display to the public some of the material we had collected, of which the nucleus was the archive of Sir Henry Irving, presented with great faith and generosity by his grandson, Laurence Irving, our first Chairman.

For all of us it was a sad day when the museum in Leighton House had to close at the end of 1977, but this was the sign of our triumph, for from the very beginning we had considered ourselves a body whose task would be finished when its object of establishing a national theatre museum had been attained. This very happy result had come about, seemingly with surprising rapidity. The enthusiastic support of two successive Directors of the Victoria and Albert Museum, Sir John Pope-Hennessy and Dr. Roy Strong, and the availability of a suite of eighteenth-century rooms in Somerset House were two of the factors that led to the announcement in the House of Commons that a Theatre Museum was to be established as an autonomous museum under the aegis of the Victoria and Albert Museum. The Fine Rooms in Somerset House were later rejected in favor of more suitable premises in the Flower Market in Covent Garden, and it is there that the Theatre Museum will open its doors to the public, it is hoped, in 1983 or 1984.

Its purpose fulfilled, the British Theatre Museum Association "committed suicide" in 1977 after transferring its collection to the Theatre Museum and its other assets to the newly-formed Friends of the Theatre Museum. Thus, twenty years after helping its birth, I officiated at its demise. But, taking another view, its achievement lives on in the new Theatre Museum. I and several of my former colleagues were invited to sit on the Advisory Committee for this new museum, and I myself derive a particular satisfaction from the thought that ballet features prominently in its exhibition policy. One of its earliest exhibitions was devoted to the career of Adeline Genée, to commemorate the centenary of her birth in 1978, but the first major declaration of the new museum's presence was the exhibition of ballet costume, "Spotlight," held in the Victoria and Albert Museum in the summer of 1981. I was responsible for the eighteenth and nineteenth century section, with Roy Strong selecting the earlier material, and Richard Buckle taking care of the twentieth century.

Pride of place among the exhibits was given to some unique eighteenth century dance costumes discovered by the museum's imaginative curator, Alexander Schouvaloff, in a palazzo in Italy. Their acquisition for the museum was a truly spectacular coup. These precious garments, saved only in the nick of time, for they were disintegrating fast, were brought back to London, one or two at a time, in the boot of Alexander's car. He told me he had his answer ready if questioned by an over-officious customs man—"Only some old clothes."

Many of the costumes exhibited were from the Diaghilev period, and had come to the museum from Richard Buckle's "Museum of the Performing Arts," a group of benefactors who had purchased them for the nation when they came on to the market. Others represented the Ballets Russes of the 1930s, and there were many from the Royal Ballet, which was celebrating its golden jubilee that year. On the walls were items from the Rambert Collection of Romantic ballet prints, another important component in the new museum's collection. Unfortunately it proved impossible to show any original costumes from the nineteenth century, but the period was honorably represented by the replica of Fanny Elssler's *Cachucha* costume which Ann had had made for the film record of her reconstruction of that dance, elegantly and expressively performed by Margaret Barbieri.

CHAPTER SEVEN

My Fanny Elssler Period

I AM often asked how long it takes me to write a book—a question I generally find hard to answer without giving a misleading impression. Usually I am only writing one book at a time, but that is only the final phase of a much larger operation, for writing cannot start until the research has reached an advanced stage, and at any one time I am collecting material for numerous projects, some of which, for one reason or another, never come to fruition.

My *Romantic Ballet in Paris,* for example, was more than fifteen years in preparation from the germination of the idea to publication. This book was part of the grand design I conceived soon after I began to study the history of the Paris Opéra, and took shape as a companion volume to my study of the ballet of the Second Empire. I must have begun to collect material for it at least as early as 1950, and over the years, as I systematically worked through the papers at the Archives Nationales and the press of the period, my folders of notes swelled. It was some years before I had enough material to begin writing the first draft, and about four chapters were roughly written when I interrupted these labors to work on my biography of Genée. Other distractions then followed, including a monograph on

Zambelli and a catalogue of Marie Rambert's collection of Romantic ballet prints, and several more years passed before I resumed work on it seriously. I eventually completed it in 1964, and it was published in 1965.

This long drawn-out period of gestation was very beneficial, for it not only gave me time to digest the vast quantity of detailed information I had amassed, but also, and more importantly, enabled me to give deeper thought to the essential nature of the Romantic movement as it affected ballet. In my early years too little emphasis had been given to interpreting the trends and influences that have affected ballet. This was perhaps inevitable in the circumstances of my own development, for when I started writing few histories could be relied on for factual accuracy and it was essential to devote a great amount of time to marshaling facts. This state of affairs still exists, because most of the subjects I have chosen have not been researched in depth before, but now, with greater experience, I feel able to draw conclusions which were beyond my capacity in my early years. The truth is that my development as a dance historian has been somewhat haphazard, for apart from my chronicles of the Paris Opéra ballet, I have had no consistent overall plan for a life's work, but have followed my enthusiasms as they took hold of me. If I were asked to recommend a plan for the education of the complete dance historian, I would of course prescribe several years spent studying the history of the dance and allied subjects in general before any specialization, but I am glad I did not have to undergo such a régime myself, for I would have foregone so much enjoyment and I am sure my writing would have lost vigor as a result.

When *The Romantic Ballet in Paris* was published, the Harvard Theatre Collection honored me by arranging an important exhibition on the Romantic ballet that featured my book and Edwin Binney's study of Théophile Gautier and his ballets, which came out at about the same time. Harvard had come to figure quite largely in my life after my marriage, for Ann's family had traditionally sent their sons there for many generations and since she is a great-granddaughter of Longfellow, we enjoyed the rare privilege of staying in the Longfellow House whenever we visited Cambridge. On our honeymoon visit to the States in 1962 we discovered the Harvard Theatre Collection, whose curator, Helen D. Willard, quickly became a very dear friend. Driving out to Cape Cod with her to spend a weekend together, we told her about the Sergeyev collection of notated ballet scores which its owner, Mona Inglesby, was wishing to sell. This unique archive, comprising virtually the entire repertory of the St. Petersburg ballet in the 1900s, had been brought out of Russia during the Revolution by the *régisseur* Nicolai Sergeyev, who had made use of it to stage revivals of the classical ballet, mostly for British companies, the Vic-Wells Ballet and, in his last years, International Ballet. When he died in 1951, all his papers became the property of International Ballet's director, Mona Inglesby. Ann and I were given a privileged glimpse of some of this material when I tried, unsuccessfully, to steer the collection to the British Theatre Museum, and with our complementary expertises we were perhaps uniquely qualified to judge its value as an archive. Realizing it was unlikely to find a home in Britain, I felt justified in advising Helen Willard that she should try to acquire it for Harvard, where it would be properly conserved and catalogued and made available to scholars. As a result of our discussion, negotiations were opened and, following a professional appraisal of the content of the notation scores by Ann, a single ballet, *Swan Lake,* was purchased, the remainder of the archive being bought a few years later.

Ed Binney, whose book shared the place of honor in Harvard's exhibition with my own, has for many years given the most valuable support, often anonymously, to the Theatre Collection. He has made considerable contributions to ballet scholarship: apart from his Gautier studies, he has compiled catalogues of nineteenth-century German and Italian ballet prints and has amassed an exceptional collection of prints, his Taglioni section being certainly the most comprehensive ever assembled. Ours is another friendship which began, some twenty years ago now, in the Library of the Opéra. He was then on a whirlwind tour researching for his doctoral thesis on Gautier's ballets, and we cemented our friendship in appropriate Second Empire surroundings, dining at the Pré Catalan in the Bois de Boulogne. During his travels he had accumulated a vast amount of notes, and now, with the day of his return to America approaching, he was making use of every moment in a frenzied effort to complete his research. I could understand his determination to consult all the authorities on his list, but I could also appreciate his wife Alicia's long-suffering support. His daily routine began when the Bibliothèque Nationale opened in the morning and continued until closing time, and to save precious minutes in the middle of the day Alicia was instructed to position herself in the Place Louvois with sandwiches ready so that he could rush out of the Library, gobble them down, and still digesting them, disappear through the portals back to his seat in the reading room.

A few weeks later this dynamo of a man passed through England on his journey home, and came to dine with us at Bickley. He brought with him photocopies of the music of the Second Empire ballet *Sacountala,* which he played with (if he will forgive me for saying so) more verve than accuracy on our piano. This was the evening he had the shock of his life on encountering our pet goat reclining in the hall. My handling of this beast of dangerous aspect made an indelible impression on him, and he seems to have dined out on the experience ever since!

My marriage had perforce changed my traveling habits, and my visits to Paris became less frequent as I began to discover and love America. In New York there was Lillian Moore to look up, and the evenings we spent with her in her West 46th Street apartment— sometimes sharing the dining table with her very sleek and very spoiled Burmese cats!—have become memories which I cherish now with a feeling of poignant nostalgia, for in 1967 she died, before her time, of cancer. Her death was a great blow, for our friendship was founded on a mutual respect for one another's work and a selfless willingness to share our discoveries. Fanny Elssler, who was the subject of Lillian's first article, and on whose biography I was now about to embark, was a heroine to both of us, and one of Lillian's last gestures was to allow me to photograph one of her most treasured possessions—a portrait of the dancer and her son, painted on porcelain, which she had bought, paying the purchase price by a long series of installments while the dealer retained the picture. The last time I saw Lillian was in the summer of 1966, as she sprang into a bus and waved goodbye with a jaunty peaked cap on her head. How fitting that I should have been left with an image of a dancer rather than a scholar, for her writing came alive for the very reason that it was founded on the physical experience of a dancer's toil and satisfaction.

I was very grieved that she would never be able to read my biography of Elssler, which I dedicated to her memory when it was published in 1970. The idea for this book had been germinating in my mind for a long time. Fanny Elssler had fascinated me ever since I had come across Henry Wikoff's *Reminiscences of an Idler* when researching for my book on Napoleon III. Wikoff had played an important part in Elssler's famous American tour, and his recollections of the ballerina, which had escaped the notice of her biographers, had led me to write a series of articles on her and her friends for *Ballet* in the late 1940s. Before embarking on a full-length biography, however, I had to "fall out of love" with Fanny Cerrito, with whom Elssler had had an historic contest on the stage of Her Majesty's Theatre in 1843, when the two ballerinas battled for supremacy in a *pas de deux* arranged specially for them by Perrot. I had described this from the viewpoint of a Cerrito enthusiast, and I now had to switch my loyalty. By 1965 nearly ten years had passed since I had written the last word of my book on Cerrito, and I felt emotionally ready to devote myself to her one-time rival.

With Cerrito I had been working in virgin soil, but in the case of Elssler other biographers had preceded me. The first, and in my opinion the best, was Auguste Ehrhard, whose book had been published as long ago as 1909, truly a vintage year for it saw also Dacier's classic biography of Marie Sallé—and, of course, Diaghilev's first season of ballet in Paris. A grimmer year, 1940, had seen the appearance of Emil Pirchan's biography, a work that was somewhat light in the text but contained a wealth of illustrations even if some of them were not of Elssler at all. And shortly before my own book came out, Riki Raab, who had herself been a distinguished dancer at the Vienna State Opera, wrote an excellent biography. Each of these books had its merits, but none of them to my mind gave a balanced picture of Elssler's international career or fully explained her significance in the history of ballet, as it was my intention to do.

To achieve this, it was necessary to comb the available archives and make an exhaustive examination of the newspapers and periodicals of Vienna, Paris, London, Milan, Berlin, St. Petersburg, Moscow, a whole string of towns and cities in America and Cuba, and elsewhere. I could never have done this entirely on my own, and the acknowledgments in my book show how much a conscientious historian working on a broad canvas must rely on the good will and cooperation of others, and particularly on colleagues specializing in areas closely related to his subject.

The highlights of Elssler's career were the two years she spent in the United States and Cuba and the visits she made to Russia at the end of her career, and these I was able to cover in great detail thanks to the generosity of fellow scholars. For the American scene, my chief benefactor was Allison Delarue of Princeton. He had written a full-length study of Henry Wikoff which he lent me in typescript, together with all the notes on which it had been based, with permission to use whatever I needed. This was an incredibly generous gesture which I fully appreciated. Allison's material provided me with a solid framework on which to build my chapters on the American visit, enabling me to follow Fanny as she traveled across America in the days when farmers drove their pigs along the streets of

New York, Indian wars were still raging in Florida, and communications were very primitive. I was able to weave into this part of the story many personal details culled from a fascinating series of letters which Fanny's cousin and companion, Katti Prinster, wrote to her family back in Austria. Then for the Russian seasons, I was privileged to have the cooperation of four distinguished Russian historians, who had become friends as well as colleagues through correspondence. Yuri Bakhrushin lent me the typescript of a long essay on Elssler's visits to Russia, and Yuri Slonimsky, Vera Krasovskaya and Natalia Roslavleva each provided me with references, arranged for material in Russia to be copied for me, and patiently answered many enquiries.

The reading and organization of these materials in many different languages was no small task. While I am not a natural linguist, I was able to cope with several of these languages myself. French poses no difficulties, Russian I can translate at a reasonable speed with a dictionary, and I can pick my way through most Latin languages, although here I need help with literary forms and difficult passages. My wife's favorite cousin, Maria Calderón, who was studying Romance languages at London University at the time, turned the chore of translating Italian into pure joy. Her silvery laughter rippled through the flat as she translated the waffly effusions of minor Italian poets, and her pronunciation of the name of Cerrito was so musical that I nearly fell in love with that dancer all over again! The one major language that defeated me completely was German, and here I was fortunate in being able to call upon Stuart Barker, a balletomane of long standing who for some two years came to dinner once a week, afterwards spending a couple of hours before the microfilm reader, dictating his translation into the tape recorder. The value of such modern aids, including the ubiquitous Xerox machine, has not only made the historian's task incalculably easier, but has brought within his reach a quantity of material that was virtually denied to scholars not many generations ago. It is a little humbling to reflect that our successors, who may be able to retrieve source material at the press of a button on some sort of desk computer, will think of us as primitive pioneers!

At the time I was writing my book on Elssler, Ann was working herself to a shadow on the second edition of her definitive textbook on Labanotation, and with notators and typists on hand, our flat became such a hive of activity that many of our more conventional friends must have thought we were well on the way to the asylum! As the tempo of writing stepped up, I would proclaim ''Fanny

Elssler days,'' when everything had to give place to concentrated work on the book.

They were hectic but stimulating times, producing moments of true elation at an exciting discovery or some experience that brought me closer to my subject. When I was researching in Vienna, I was able to see and touch Fanny's *Cachucha* costume, its material still crisp and the colors still vivid and fresh. Then there were delightful visits to Eisenstadt, the quiet little town in Bergenland where the composer Haydn is buried. One of the streets there is named after Fanny Elssler, and there is a collection of her personal relics in the Haydn Museum.

Another unforgettable journey was to Salzburg, to visit Friderica Derra de Moroda, a scholar of dance history whose knowledge was unrivaled, as also was her library which, on her death in 1978, was bequeathed to the University of Salzburg. Her knowledge was always most generously placed at the disposal of scholars whose work she respected, and being fortunate enough to fall within that category, I gathered many rare pieces of information about Fanny Elssler during the few days I spent as her guest.

Back at home there was another memorable day when I confirmed the date of birth of Fanny Elssler's daughter Therese. I had written to all the Catholic churches that had existed in London in 1834, and from one of the priests came the reply that he had traced the entry of the baptism in his registers and that Fanny and her sister had given false names, which later had to be corrected when the girl reached full age and needed to prove her birth in connection with a settlement of property. This fascinating, but minor, discovery reached me on a Saturday when I was beset with anxiety over a crisis that had arisen at the R.A.D., and helped take my mind off that problem.

Fanny Elssler came out almost simultaneously with a spate of lesser works: a booklet on *Coppélia* which I wrote for the Friends of Covent Garden to commemorate that ballet's centenary, an essay on the *Pas de Quatre* to accompany a facsimile edition of the piano score, a lighthearted piece about *Dandies and Dancers* in early nineteenth-century London for *Dance Perspectives,* and a biography of Carlotta Zambelli.

The work on Zambelli, which I had written nearly ten years earlier, was the most substantial of these. Although comparatively short, it was a detailed account of her long career as ballerina and teacher at the Opéra, set against the history of French ballet during a period that had received little attention from historians. Zambelli's

home in Paris was the same fourth-floor apartment she had moved
into on her first engagement in 1894, and I often climbed the stairs
to lunch with her and listen to her reminiscences. I also spent many
an interval at the Opéra, sitting by her side on a bench in the corridor by the entrance to the *parterre* where she and Aveline had their
seats. Aveline, who had been her partner for many years and was
one of the *maîtres de ballet* at the Opéra, was—in Zambelli's
presence—a mild, retiring man with a perpetual look of naive wonder and very little to say. The two were inseparable, but their relationship was apparently wholly platonic. The same sort of bond
united them as exists between twins. For when Zambelli died in
Milan in January 1968, Aveline was lying ill at his home in Asnières
and died a few days later without having been told of her death.
Paulette Dynalix, who was a pupil of Zambelli and had so often
heard her summon Aveline with the cry of "Avelin! Avelin!" (pro-
nouncing it always as if it lacked the final "e"), imagined the scene
when Zambelli arrived at the gates of Heaven. "Avelin, hurry up,
I'm waiting!" went out the familiar call when she found herself
alone, and inevitably the answer came back: "I'm coming, I'm
coming, Zambell."

I felt very sad that Zambelli did not live to see my work published. I was also disconcerted to discover that I had nodded in
accepting without question the date of her birth, as given by all the
reference books and not corrected by her when I checked the details
of her birth and baptism. With my experience of Cerrito deducting
four years from her age, I should have known better. For soon after
my work was first published, in French, by the Société d'Histoire
du Théâtre, André Ménetrat wrote to me that Zambelli's nieces had
told him their aunt was born in 1875, not 1877. Belatedly I obtained
a copy of her birth certificate, which confirmed the earlier date. I
was happily able to make a correction in the English version of my
monograph, which *Dance Magazine* published in 1974, but it taught
me a lesson never to take for granted a lady's statement about her
age.

CHAPTER EIGHT

Virginia Zucchi... and After

NOT long before he died in 1963, Cyril Swinson, being depressed about the declining market for serious books on ballet and forced to consider cutting down Blacks' unrivaled ballet list, told me I should take the philosophical view that I had written the specialized books that were in me while the going was good. As events proved, his foreboding was unfounded, for shortly after his death, with the growing acceptance of dance as an educational subject, there was a resurgence of interest. It was a tragedy that he did not live to see this, not merely for his own sake, but because he would have been uniquely qualified to represent the publishing profession in this development.

So there has been a modest enough demand for specialized books, and I have continued along the largely untrodden byways of dance history with sufficient prospect of my work appearing in print to give me the necessary incentive. This is important because my books of their very nature have to be written at my own speed and, except on very rare occasions, I do not even set myself a target date for completion, let alone sign a contract in advance with a deadline for the manuscript to be delivered.

A work that gestated longer than most was a collection of the correspondence of Arthur Saint-Léon, the choreographer of *Coppélia*. Saint-Léon had the misfortune to be ballet master in Russia between the spells of two greater figures, Jules Perrot and Marius Petipa, whose genius has overshadowed his own efforts, with the result that history has judged him less favorably than he deserved. He was certainly not a great choreographer in the sense that Perrot was, but if his ballets were not cohesive dramatic entities, they were full of joyous dancing, as evidenced by the traditional version of *Coppélia* given at the Paris Opéra. I had stumbled across Saint-Léon the man in the early days of my researches at the Archives Nationales, discovering letter after letter he wrote to his friend Charles Nuitter. They were wonderfully vivid and warmly personal, and I quoted from them extensively in my *Ballet of the Second Empire*. These extracts, however, amounted only to a small proportion of the whole correspondence, and on reading the letters again while preparing my booklet on *Coppélia,* I realized that they gave a unique view of ballet in Paris, St. Petersburg and Moscow in the 1860s and should be made available to students of the period. I had unearthed forty letters at the Archives Nationales, and as a result of a wider search I was able to locate another twenty-three elsewhere. Inevitably, I felt, some of the flavor of these letters would be lost if translated out of their original French, and so I offered the collection to the Société d'Histoire du Théâtre, preceded by a long article on Saint-Léon and the importance of his career, with detailed annotations and a list of his ballets and music compositions. Publication was delayed on account of the Molière tercentenary which seemed to absorb all available space in the Société's journal quite interminably, but at last it came out, early in 1978, under the title *Lettres d'un maître de ballet.*

After *Fanny Elssler* was published I transferred my affections to Virginia Zucchi—to the distress, I think, of my valued friend and colleague, Marian Hannah Winter, who thought I should be concentrating on my Paris Opéra history. But no one had written a biography of Zucchi, who had exerted such a hypnotic influence not only on Benois and other colleagues of Diaghilev, but on the generation of Russian dancers who graced the Imperial Ballet at its apogee at the end of the nineteenth century. It was clear to me that her significance was much greater than she had been given credit for, and when G. B. L. Wilson commented one day on the paucity of pictures of her, I decided to take up the challenge. Another spur was a chance meeting, in 1962, with her niece, Mrs. Virginia Hackett, arranged through the kindness of Walter Terry, the American dance critic, who happened to know her son. Mrs. Hackett had received me very graciously in her elegant New York apartment and had spoken at length about her aunt. I had made notes of our talk, which I filed away for future use. The intention to write a book on Zucchi must have formed itself soon afterwards, and my file on her grew fuller as I warmed to the task. From the French newspapers I pieced together a picture of her triumph at the Eden-Théâtre in Paris, and her interviews with Parisian journalists gave me an illuminating insight into her early career and her personal life, for she was an endearingly uninhibited romanticist. Meanwhile my Russian friends were responding generously to requests for information, and the day eventually arrived when my instinct told me that it was time to start writing.

Now the era of "Virginia Zucchi Days" began! But I realized almost at once there were still wide gaps to fill, particularly in my knowledge of her activities in Italy, where she had begun her career and danced regularly until her retirement. There are many excellent histories of Italian theatres, but generally these give only basic factual information and I knew I would have to work systematically through the Italian theatrical press if I were to do justice to her appearances in her native country. It was a daunting task, for I would have to begin my search in the mid-1860s to pinpoint her stage début and work my way through to her retirement around 1900, a span of more than thirty years. So fundamental was this research that it was out of the question to delegate it to anyone else, however competent, and I decided to visit Milan to undertake a "crash program." Through John Field, who was then director of the ballet at the Scala, I was fortunate in having the help of Lisa Finzi, one of the dancers there who spoke fluent English. Lisa not only facilitated my research at the Museum of La Scala, but also undertook a number of assignments after my return to London. The center of my activities in Milan was the Biblioteca Braidense, where I worked every day from opening to closing without wasting any time for lunch. I had steeled myself in advance to meet with frustration and even to returning to London with only part of my task accomplished. But in fact I could not have met with greater cooperation or efficiency. The bound volumes of periodicals I required were brought to my table rapidly and in the numbers I needed, and at the end of my visit my large microfilm order was carried out within twenty-four hours. So tight was my schedule that I had to discipline myself very firmly to note only the references relating to Zucchi—

not an easy task when there was so much of interest to me on the pages that passed before my eyes—but the length of my visit proved to have been nicely gauged and I returned to London having worked through all the material on my list.

My search for Virginia Zucchi's descendants had of course begun with Mrs. Hackett. However, when I was ready to follow up the information she had given me I found, to my sorrow, that she had died a few years before. How much I have regretted not keeping in touch with her while I was working on other books, for I would have learned so much that is now lost forever. Mrs. Hackett, who had been a ballerina herself, had been trained by her aunt, and I had not begun to enquire into this. Mea culpa, mea culpa! What a lesson there is in this misfortune—how important to seize one's opportunities as they arise!

Fortunately I was able to trace Mrs. Hackett's children and her sister. Her daughter, Mrs. Carla Quijano, was particularly helpful, writing to me at great length and very vividly about her memories of her great-aunt and lending me some fascinating family photographs. But there still remained one mystery to be unraveled before I could consider my task complete—the whereabouts of Virginia Zucchi's descendants. Mrs. Hackett had told me that Zucchi had had a daughter, Marie, by an artist called Jourdan, and that Marie's daughter had married a Monsieur Braun, the proprietor of two restaurants in Paris between the wars. But the American branch of the family had lost touch with them many years before, and Mrs. Quijano could tell me no more.

My early efforts to identify the mysterious Jourdan proved fruitless. Several artists of that name were listed in the reference books, and it was of course possible that Zucchi's husband or lover—I knew not which, although I suspected the latter since her death certificate described her as "célibataire"—had not been distinguished enough to merit mention. If only I could trace the entry of Marie's birth I might find a lead, but I knew neither when nor where she was born. It was Mrs. Quijano who gave me the first clue, telling me Marie had married a Dr. Lacaze who owned property in the Ardèche. In the hope that the date of her birth might be recorded on her tomb, I wrote to the local curé to seek his help. He replied that Mme. Lacaze did not appear to be buried in his parish, and it seemed I had reached a dead end in more senses than one! Then, more than six months later, a letter arrived from a Charles Braun of Zurich, saying that the curé had been in touch with him and that he was Virginia Zucchi's great-grandson. At first he seemed a little offended by my interest in his great-grandmother's private life, but he gave me the information I needed to obtain Marie's birth certificate and to identify Monsieur Jourdan. Charles Braun's attitude of reserve apparently stemmed partly from the conclusion I had reached that Zucchi and Jourdan were never married. In the end I sent him a copy of my final chapter, which convinced him of the serious intention of my work, for he thanked me very warmly and made a number of helpful suggestions.

Although in the course of my researches I have often wandered far from the Paris Opéra, that august institution has remained my spiritual home and whenever I am in Paris it is always my first port of call. I was always assured of a warm welcome from the many friends I had made there, but there came a time, in the early 1970s, when all those dignified officials reached retiring age. They all seemed to depart at once, and I became apprehensive that the links I had forged over so many years might be broken. But my fears proved groundless, for I discovered that the Opéra was filled with enthusiastic men and women of a generation younger than myself who made me feel part of the theatre more than ever before. It was a strange experience, for my standing seemed to change, without any transition, from that of a young scholar to that of a visiting dignitary!

When I was asked, in 1974, to write the history of the Paris Opéra ballet, no greater compliment could have been paid to me. I like to think of it as a recognition of the many, many hours I had spent—in obedience to my obsession, and without thought of reward—piecing together the story of the theatre's past, and I appreciated that the honor was all the greater in being offered to one who was not a Frenchman. Without waiting for a formal contract I threw myself wholeheartedly into the task. As was to be expected, the early chapters took longer than the others, for although I had collected a great quantity of information, I had not absorbed it as I had the material on the nineteenth century. When I was in my stride, however, I was writing at the rate of a chapter a month, and to speed up the process of publication I sent the chapters, three or four at a time, to Paris to be translated. My reluctance to commit myself to a deadline had been understandingly accepted by the Opéra, but I set myself the target date for which they had asked and had the satisfaction of delivering the last chapter some weeks before the deadline that had originally been suggested. It was not until after the book had been written and delivered that the contract was signed.

As I write these last pages my desk is beginning to creak under the weight of paper that represents my work in progress, a biography of the greatest choreographer of Romantic times, Jules Perrot. It is taking shape in the same way as have all the other books I have written. Each chapter is first drafted, very roughly, in manuscript. In this first stage I am following the precept which I learned from a wise friend when I was a boy—get something down on paper and do not worry about style. Next, I polish this first draft to make it readable, adding, cutting, correcting and rewriting, and from this draft I type a fair copy which becomes my working draft. This working draft grows chapter by chapter, and the book takes its natural shape in the course of writing, for I do not construct it to a precise plan worked out in advance, although I do have in my mind from the beginning an idea of its form, which is, of course, adapted during the writing process as the results of further research require. Once this working draft is complete, the task of serious revision begins, and the once-clear typescript pages become overlaid with a jumble of deletions, corrections, corrections of corrections, insertions on slips of paper gummed at the side, not to mention the occasional doodle when inspiration has momentarily flagged! From this heavily mutilated draft the final typescript is prepared—a task I invariably do myself because it gives me a last opportunity of adding polish and also, occasionally, picking up an error which had previously escaped me. I like to think that the final result will read as flowingly as a work of fiction springing inspirationally from a novelist's pen, betraying none of the toil of its construction.

Although the removal of visible seams may not be completed until the final revision, the secret of presenting the narrative coherently is to be sought further back in the earliest stages, in the ability to control the vast amount of material on which the book is based. This depends largely on the organization of one's filing system and one's efficiency in retrieving information from it. To be methodical is a cardinal rule for every historian, but each of us has his or her own methods. In my own case the system has grown up to suit my particular needs, and it can only be judged subjectively. The basic files in my cabinets are divided into cities (London, Paris) and countries (Russia, Italy, Austria, Denmark, etc.), and in some cases subdivided into periods and even, in the case of the London and Paris files, individual years. Then there are subject files dealing with general matters such as ballet music, and files containing material which I have used for my books and which does not naturally find its place in the basic files. Thus there are three large files on Elssler, four on Cerrito and five on Zucchi. Now Jules Perrot has a growing file to himself, containing material not to be found in the files on ballet in London, Paris, Italy and Russia. And now I have a confession to make. I do not have a cross-referencing index, but rely on my memory and my familiarity with the contents of my filing cabinets. This may sound disgracefully haphazard, but it works and I have, therefore, always begrudged time spent on filling out cards.

To return to my work on Perrot, this was undertaken at the pressing suggestion of the Soviet ballet historian, Yuri Slonimsky, with whom I had a long correspondence extending over some twenty years. As a result of the privations he had suffered during the Siege of Leningrad, his last years were clouded by ill health and his working capacity grew less and less, causing him great frustration, for his mind was still conjuring up new projects which he could never realize. Jules Perrot was very close to his heart—he had produced a perceptive essay on him just before World War II—and when he suggested I should write the biography which, given better health, he would have himself written, I decided to put other plans aside to make way for it. In the last year of his life—he died in March 1978—he supplied me with much valuable material on Perrot's years in Russia and sent me a flow of questions, comments and suggestions in his letters. He knew he would never live to read the book, which must now be dedicated to his memory.

I have subtitled these pages ''An Unfinished Memoir'' because I hope to spend many more years discovering and re-creating the past. My grand design of chronicling French ballet in detail has so far covered only half a century—1820 to 1870—and I am now contemplating a further installment that will carry the story back through the period of the Gardel brothers, and possibly to the difficult years which Noverre spent at the Opéra as the protégé of Marie-Antoinette. This, I hope, will be seen as complementing the remarkable study on *The Pre-Romantic Ballet* by Marian Hannah Winter in somewhat the same way as my *Romantic Ballet in Paris* supplemented the survey of that period which she gave in her other great work, *Le Théâtre du Merveilleux*. Hannah and I knew one another for more than twenty years, and I spent many a happy hour in her company discussing our work and listening to her inexhaustible supply of anecdotes and gossip which she would recount with irrepressible verve. In the field of dance history there was no more remarkable scholar than she. She was an original in the true sense of the word, original in the thought that penetrates her work, original in her view of ballet as linked with the other arts of spectacle, and original in her unremitting quest for the raw material she needed for her work—manuscripts, books and above all pictorial records—in the face of difficulties which would make an ordinary mortal quail. She shed more new light on the development of eighteenth century ballet than any other historian. Among her contributions to knowledge was to have brought to light again the career of Pierre Gardel, who was all-powerful in the Paris ballet for several decades. Gardel will be a principal character—whether or not the hero must remain to be seen—in this projected new work of mine, and I shall feel honored to have my name coupled with that of Hannah, who died in 1981, in the doing of justice to this forgotten artist.

Another French choreographer of the eighteenth century is beginning to awaken my interest—Jean Dauberval, creator of *La Fille mal gardée*. Over the years I have noted down numerous references to his life and career which lie in my files waiting to be taken out to become the springboard for more concentrated research.

What, the reader may now ask, no more dead ballerinas? Well, I must confess to a fondness for a forgotten figure of the past—Adèle Grantzow, a jinx if ever there was, but that is another story—and an interest in the great teacher who formed her and many other dancers of the French school of the nineteenth century, Madame Dominique.

An historian's life is never a dull one, for his world is continually expanding as he conjures up figures out of the past who appear to him almost as real as his flesh-and-blood contemporaries. In the hall of our flat is a large and very lovely photograph of Virginia Zucchi, and one evening, as I was quietly working at my desk, I heard Ann greeting some of her students who had come to see her notation materials. One of them noticed the picture and commented on it.

"That," said Ann in a very matter-of-fact tone, "is the woman my husband is in love with."

I could sense the moment of awful embarrassment that followed this remark, until Ann, with perfect timing, released the tension.

"But don't worry," she added. "You see, she has been dead these forty years."

I smiled. Only an historian, I thought, can lead a double life with such impunity!

Ivor Guest: A Chronology

1920   April 14. Born in Chislehurst, Kent, England.

1933–38   Educated at Lancing College, after preparatory education in
              Littlehampton, Sussex.

1938–40   Studied Law at Trinity College, Cambridge (Master of Arts).

1940–46   Served in the British Army (Northern Ireland, France, Belgium,
              Holland, Germany).

1946   First article on ballet history published in *Ballet* (December is-
              sue).

1949   Admitted a Solicitor.

1951   Became a partner in the firm of A.F. & R.W. Tweedie.

1952   First book published, *Napoleon III in England.*
              Joined the editorial board of *The Ballet Annual* as Associate Edi-
              tor, remaining on board until the last issue in 1964.

1953   *The Ballet of the Second Empire, 1858–70*

1954   *The Romantic Ballet in England*

1955   *The Ballet of the Second Empire, 1847–58*
        Elected to the Committee of the Society for Theatre Research
        (until 1972).

1956   *Fanny Cerrito. The Story of a Romantic Ballerina*

1957   Organized National Book League exhibition of books on ballet.
        Appointed Adviser on Ballet to the *Enciclopedia dello Spetta-
        colo.*
        Victorian Ballet-Girl. The Tragic Story of Clara Webster.
        Appointed Honorary Legal Adviser to the British Theatre Mu-
        seum Association on its foundation.

1958   *Adeline Genée. A Lifetime of Ballet under Six Reigns*

1959   Advised on musical sources for Frederick Ashton's *La Fille mal
        gardée* (produced January 1960), discovering the original
        score.
        The Alhambra Ballet

1960   *La Fille mal Gardée* (as editor and contributor).
        The Dancer's Heritage. A Short History of Ballet

1962   January 20. Married Ann Hutchinson at St. George's Church,
        Bickley, Kent.
        The Empire Ballet

1963   Appointed Editorial Adviser to *The Dancing Times.*

1965   Elected to the Executive Committee of the Royal Academy of
        Dancing (January).
        A Gallery of Romantic Ballet

1966   Elected Vice-Chairman of the British Theatre Museum Associa-
        tion (until 1977).
        Appointed Secretary of the Radcliffe Trust.
        Harvard Theatre Collection exhibition on the Romantic Ballet
        featured *The Romantic Ballet in Paris.*
        The Romantic Ballet in Paris

1969   Elected Chairman of the Royal Academy of Dancing (November 11).
        Dandies and Dancers
        Carlotta Zambelli

1969–70 Acted as Historical Adviser to Ballet for All's centenary production, *The Two Coppélias.*

1970   *Two Coppélias. A Centenary Study*
        Fanny Elssler. The Pagan Ballerina
        The Pas de Quatre

1974   Appointed a member of the Theatre Museum Advisory Council.

1976   *Le Ballet de l'Opéra de Paris. Trois siècles d'histoire et de tradition*

1977   *The Divine Virginia. A Biography of Virginia Zucchi*
        Lettres d'un Maître de Ballet

1978   *Adeline Genée. A Pictorial Record*

1978–80 Acted as Historical Adviser to the BBC television series, *The Magic of Dance,* by Margot Fonteyn.

1980–81 Acted as Adviser on the 18th and 19th century sections of the exhibition "Spotlight," presented by the Theatre Museum in the Victoria & Albert Museum.

1981   *Costume and the 19th Century Dancer* (contribution to Designing for the Dancer).
        Fanny Elssler's Cachucha (as contributor)

Bibliography

1946   " 'Coppélia' 1870." *Ballet,* 2, No. 7 (Dec. 1946), 41–46.

1947   "The Ballet-girl of 1847." *Ballet,* 4, No. 6 (Dec. 1947), 29–36.
"Bal Mabille." *Ballet,* 3, No. 2 (Feb. 1947), 39–44.
"The Eglinton Tournament." *Ballet,* 4, No. 2 (Aug. 1947), 29–36.
"Fanny Elssler and her Friends—Part I. Henry Wikoff." *Ballet,* 4, No. 5 (Nov. 1947), 44–49.
"The Fire at Covent Garden." *Ballet,* 3, No. 3 (Mar.–Apr. 1947), 43–48.
" 'Giselle' as an Opera and the Opera Burlesqued." *Ballet,* 4, No. 4 (Oct. 1947), 13–18.
"More about Emma Palladino." *Ballet,* 4, No. 2 (Aug. 1947), 59–60.

1948   "Babbage's Ballet." *Ballet,* 5, No. 4 (Apr. 1948), 51–56.
"Cora Pearl Plays Cupid." *Ballet,* 5, No. 5 (May 1948), 40–46.
"Fanny Elssler and her Friends—Part II. Friedrich von Gentz." *Ballet,* 5, No. 6 (June 1948), 32–36.
"Fanny Elssler and her Friends—Part III. Mrs. Grote." *Ballet,* 6, No. 1 (Oct. 1948), 38–43.
" 'La Sylphide' in London." *Ballet and Opera,* 6, No. 3 (Dec. 1948), 39–45.

"Napoleon III and the Ballet." *Ballet*, 5, No. 2 (Feb. 1948), 38–44.

"A Note on Giselle." *Ballet*, 5, No. 5 (May 1948), 13–16.

"Who was Madame Angot?" *Ballet*, 5, No. 1 (Jan. 1948), 16–18.

1949　　"Ballet News: France." *Ballet and Opera*, 8, No. 2 (Aug. 1949), 31–34.

"Ballet News: France." *Ballet and Opera*, 8, No. 3 (Sept. 1949), 41–44.

"Clara Webster." *Ballet and Opera*, 8, No. 4 (Oct. 1949), 15–20.

"New Year 1812." *Ballet and Opera*, 7, No. 1 (Jan. 1949), 25–28.

"Stage Designers—VI. Pierre Ciceri." *Ballet and Opera*, 8, No. 1 (July 1949), 20–28.

1950　　"The Ceremony at Vestris' Tomb, Paris, July 23." *Ballet*, 10, No. 2 (Sept.–Oct. 1950), 51.

"A Hundred Years Ago: Ballet in London, 1850." *Ballet*, 10, No. 3 (Nov.–Dec. 1950), 38–39.

"Notes on the Paris Opéra Repertory." *Ballet*, 10, No. 2 (Sept.–Oct. 1950), 38–42.

"The Opéra Balls." *Ballet*, 9, No. 3 (Mar. 1950), 27–33.

1951　　"The Ballet Espagnol of Pilar Lopez." *Ballet Today*, Nov. 1951, 8–10.

"Chalon at the Ballet: Caricatures with Notes." *Ballet*, 11, No. 10 (Nov. 1951), 40–47.

"Delibes' 'Sylvia.' " *Ballet*, 11, No. 2 (Mar. 1959), 18–26.

"Impressions of the Paris Opéra Ballet." *Ballet*, 11, No. 9 (Oct. 1951), 21–24.

"100 Years Ago: Ballet in London 1851." *Ballet*, 11, No. 11 (Dec. 1951), 26–29.

"The 'Pas de Quatre': Its History and a Reconstruction, with a Note on Dolin's Recent Version." *Ballet*, 11, No. 7 (Aug. 1951), 44–48.

1952　　*Apologie de la Danse* by F. de Lauze. Trans. Joan Wildeblood. [Review of.] *R.A.D. Gazette*, Aug. 1952, 18.

"Blanche-neige." [Review of first performance at the Paris Opéra, Nov. 14, 1951.] *Dance and Dancers*, 3, No. 1 (Jan. 1952), 14.

" 'Carmen' at the Alhambra." *Ballet,* 12, No. 7 (July 1952), 22–24.

"An Earlier 'Sleeping Beauty': 'La Belle au Bois Dormant' in the Eighteen Thirties." *Ballet,* 12, No. 4 (Apr. 1952), 36–42.

"The Graces." *Ballet Today,* Feb. 1952, 6–7.

" 'Gretna Green.' " *Ballet,* 12, No. 1 (Jan. 1952), 29–31.

"The Heyday of the *Cancan.*" In *Second Empire Medley.* Ed. W.H. Holden. London: British Technical and General Press, 1952. pp. 10–23.

"Impressions of the Paris Opéra Ballet." *Ballet,* 12, No. 9 (Sept. 1952), 28–31.

"The Miracles of Jules Perrot/Les Miracles de Jules Perrot." *Opera Ballet Music-Hall,* No. 2 (Winter 1952), 51–60.

Napoleon III in England. London: British Technical and General Press, 1952.

"Portraits—2. Lycette Darsonval." [Unsigned article.] *Ballet,* 12, No. 2 (Feb. 1952), 12–15.

"Queens of the Cancan; they made Paris gay." *Dance and Dancers,* 3, No. 12 (Dec. 1952), 14.

Some Historical Dances (Twelfth to Nineteenth Century), described and annotated by Melusine Wood. [Review of.] *R.A.D. Gazette,* Nov. 1952, 9.

" 'Sylvia' and the Future." *Ballet,* 12, No. 10 (Oct. 1952), 16–17.

1953   *The Ballet of the Second Empire.* Vol. II 1858–70. With a Preface by Serge Lifar. London: A. & C. Black, 1953.

"The First Swanilda: Giuseppina Bozzacchi (1853–1870)." *The Dancing Times,* No. 518 (Nov. 1953), 83–84.

"Le Foyer de la Danse." *The Ballet Annual,* 7 (1953), 56–60.

"Les Indes Galantes." *Dance and Dancers,* 4, No. 1 (Jan. 1953), 11.

"Stars of the Second Empire." *Dance and Dancers,* 4, No. 12 (Dec. 1953), 12–13.

1954   "Amalia Ferraris." *The Dancing Times,* No. 521 (Feb. 1954), 283–284.

"La Esmeralda." *Dance and Dancers,* 5, No. 7 (July 1954), 6–7.

"Fair Exchange: The Stars of the Paris Opéra." *Dance and Dancers,* 5, No. 9 (Sept. 1954), 9–11.

"One-Legged Dancers." *Dance and Dancers,* 5, No. 1 (Jan. 1954), 13.

"The Paris Opéra Ballet: A Glimpse at its Repertory." *The Dancing Times*, No. 529 (Oct. 1954), 9–11.

"The Paris Opéra Ballet Season—1952-53." *The Ballet Annual*, 8 (1954), 96–100.

"The Paris Opéra during the Second Empire." *Dance and Dancers*, 5, No. 10 (Oct. 1954), 9–11.

The Romantic Ballet in England. London: Phoenix House Ltd., 1954.

"Sylvia: From Mérante to Ashton." *The Ballet Annual*, 8 (1954), 67–71.

"The Travesty Role in 'Coppélia.' " *The Ballet Annual*, 8 (1954), 95.

1955   *The Ballet of the Second Empire.* Vol. I 1847–58. London: A. & C. Black, 1955.

"Emma Livry." *Opera Ballet Music-Hall*, No. 3 (1955), 49–52.

"An Introduction to the Paris Opéra Ballet." *The Ballet Annual*, 9 (1955), 64–70.

"The Paris Opéra Ballet Season—1953-54." *The Ballet Annual*, 9 (1955), 113–114.

"Parodies of *Giselle* on the English Stage (1841–1871)." *Theatre Notebook*, 9, No. 2 (Jan.–Mar. 1955), 38–46.

1956   "Camargo's Composer." *The Dancing Times*, No. 549 (June 1956), 508–509.

"Dame Adeline Genée." *The Ballet Annual*, 10 (1956), 54–61.

"A Dancer of the 'Nineties: Cléo de Mérode." *The Dancing Times*, No. 544 (Jan. 1956), 234.

Fanny Cerrito. The Story of a Romantic Ballerina. London: Phoenix House Ltd., 1956.

"The Paris Opéra Ballet Season—1954-55." *The Ballet Annual*, 10 (1956), 112–114.

"The Triumphs of Fanny Cerrito: The Story of One of the Ballerinas for whom Pas de Quatre was Designed." *Dance Magazine*, 26, No. 11 (Nov. 1956), 44–46, 67–69.

1957   *Ballet.* [Catalogue of] An Exhibition of Books, MSS, Playbills, Prints &c. illustrating the development of the art from its origins until modern times, organized by Ivor Guest. London: The National Book League, 7 Nov. 1957–4 Jan. 1958.

"Books on Ballet." *Books,* Oct.–Nov. 1957, 197–200.

"Great Controversy Ends." [A letter to the editor on Augusta Maywood and Maria Tallchief.] *Dance News,* December 1957.

"How the Victorian ballet-girl lived and worked." *Dance and Dancers,* 8, No. 11 (Nov. 1957), 30–31.

"The Italian Lady of Knole: Giovanna Baccelli." *The Ballet Annual,* 11 (1957), 78–85.

"Le Martyre de Saint Sébastien." *The Dancing Times,* No. 560 (May 1957), 353.

"The Paris Opéra Ballet Season—1955–56." *The Ballet Annual,* 11 (1957), 117–118.

Victorian Ballet Girl. The Tragic Story of Clara Webster. London: A. & C. Black, 1957.

1958   *Adeline Genée. A Lifetime of Ballet under Six Reigns.* London: A. & C. Black, 1958.

"Adeline Genée in America." *Dance Magazine,* 28, No. 11 (Nov. 1958), 52–55.

"The Birth of 'Coppélia.' " *Dance Magazine,* 28, No. 2 (Feb. 1958), 52–53, 67.

"Carlotta Zambelli: La Grande Mademoiselle de la Danse Française." *The Ballet Annual,* 12 (1958), 68–77.

Copinger and Skone James on the Law of Copyright. 9th ed. by F.E. Skone James and E.P. Skone James. [Review of.] *Theatre Notebook,* 13, No. 2 (Winter 1958/9), 70–71.

"Coppélia." In *World Ballet.* Ed. Arnold Haskell assisted by Mary Clarke. London: Hulton Press, 1958.

"An Early 'National' School: The Achievements of Katti Lanner." *The Dancing Times,* No. 578 (Nov. 1958), 64.

"The Paris Opéra Ballet Season—1956–57." *The Ballet Annual,* 12 (1958), 117–121.

"Les Plaisirs de l'hiver." *Dance and Dancers,* 9, No. 2 (Feb. 1958), 22–23.

"Victorian Ballet Girl." In *World Ballet.* Ed. Arnold Haskell assisted by Mary Clarke. London: Hulton Press, 1958.

1959   *Adeline Genée on Ballet.* [Script for] Recording made in London, Autumn 1959. Jupiter Recordings Ltd.

The Alhambra Ballet. Dance Perspectives, 4 (1959).

"*Undine:* The Pure Gold of Romanticism." *The Ballet Annual,* 13 (1959), 64–74.

1960   "Adeline Genée." *The Dancing Times,* No. 601 (Oct. 1960), 12.

The Dancer's Heritage. A Short History of Ballet. With a Foreword by Dame Margot Fonteyn. London: A. & C. Black, 1960.

La Fille mal Gardée. Ed. Ivor Guest. London: Dancing Times, 1960.

"La Fille mal gardée." Historical Note for Royal Ballet Programme, 1960. Revised 1977.

"Introducing 'La Fille mal Gardée.' " *The Dancing Times,* No. 593 (Feb. 1960), 240–242.

"Pas de Quatre. A Note." *Theatre Notebook,* 15, No. 2 (Winter 1960–61), 70–71.

"Romantic Ballerinas in Dublin: 1. Marie Taglioni." *Dance and Dancers,* 11, No. 3 (Mar. 1960), 22–23, 34.

"Romantic Ballerinas in Dublin: 2. Fanny Elssler." *Dance and Dancers,* 11, No. 4 (Apr. 1960), 14–15, 34.

"Romantic Ballerinas in Dublin: 3. Carlotta Grisi." *Dance and Dancers,* 11, No. 6 (June 1960), 20–21.

"Russian Dancers in London Before Diaghileff." *The Ballet Annual,* 14 (1960), 84–89.

"The Saga of La Fille mal Gardée." In *La Fille mal Gardée.* Ed. Ivor Guest. London: Dancing Times, 1960.

"Weaver's Theories." [Review of] *Famed for Dance* by Ifan Kyrle Fletcher, Selma Jeanne Cohen and Roger Lonsdale. *The Dancing Times,* No. 603 (Dec. 1960), 171.

1961   "Adeline Plunkett." *Enciclopedia dello Spettacolo* (1961).

" 'Les Deux Pigeons.' " *The Dancing Times,* No. 605 (Feb. 1961), 286–287, 309.

"From a *19th Century* Ballerina." [Letter written by Ivor Guest and signed "Yours celestially, Emma Livry," in response to an article by Lillian Moore.] *The Dancing Times,* No. 608 (May 1961), 490.

"The Legacy of Dauberval." *The Ballet Annual,* 15 (1961), 104–108.

"The Royal Academy of Dancing." Programme Note for Gala Matinee of Ballet in aid of the Royal Academy of Dancing. Theatre Royal, Drury Lane, London. 2 Nov. 1961.

"The Two Pigeons." Historical Note for Royal Ballet Programme, 1961.

"The Scores of 'La Fille Mal Gardée.' I—The Original Music."

[Written with John Lanchbery.] *Theatre Research/ Recherches Théâtrales,* 3 (1961), 32–42. "II—Herold's Score," 121–134. "III—The Royal Ballet's Score," 191–204.

1962 "Ballet Criticism: The Historian's View." *The Ballet Annual,* 16 (1962), 63–71.
The Dancer's Heritage. A Short History of Ballet. 2nd ed. London: Penguin Books, 1962.
"Daphnis and Chloë." Historical Note for Royal Ballet Programme, 1962.
The Empire Ballet. London: The Society for Theatre Research, 1962.
"Giselle." Historical Note for Royal Ballet Programme, 1962.
"The Good Humoured Ladies." Historical Note for Royal Ballet Programme, 1962.
"Le Lac des Cygnes." Historical Note for Royal Ballet Programme, 1962.
"The Pas de Quatre." *Bulletin* of the British Ballet Organisation. Part I (May 1962), 7–9; Part II (Sept. 1962), 3; Part III (Dec. 1962), 5.
"The Rite of Spring." Historical Note for Royal Ballet Programme, 1962.
"The Sleeping Beauty." Historical Note for Royal Ballet Programme, 1962.
"Les Sylphides." Historical Note for Royal Ballet Programme, 1962.

1963 "The Adventures of Albertine." *The Ballet Annual,* 17 (1963), 49–54.
"Ballet Imperial." Historical Note for Royal Ballet Programme, 1963.
"La Bayadère." Historical Note for Royal Ballet Programme, 1963.
"Mr. C.W. Swinson, Publisher and Author." [Obituary for.] *The Times.* 12 Jan. 1963.
Dancers of Mercury: The Story of Ballet Rambert by Mary Clarke. [Review of] *Theatre Notebook,* 17, No. 4 (Summer 1963), 140–142.
"Living and Learning." *Dance and Dancers,* 14, No. 3 (Mar. 1963), 9.
"Petrushka." Historical Note for Royal Ballet Programme, 1963.

"Swan Lake." Historical Note for Royal Ballet Programme, 1963.

"Swan Lake: A History." *About the House,* 1, No. 5 (Christmas 1963), 24–28.

1964   "Baronova on the Ballets Russes." *The Dancing Times,* No. 643 (Apr. 1964), 350.

"Les Biches." Historical Note for Royal Ballet Programme, 1964.

"Centenary: Emma Livry, 1842–63." *The Ballet Annual,* 18 (1964), 54–60.

"Le Corsaire" Pas de deux. Historical Note for Royal Ballet Programme, 1964.

"The Firebird." Historical Note for Royal Ballet Programme, 1964.

"Paquita Returns to Drury Lane." *The Dancing Times,* No. 651 (Dec. 1964), 127–128.

"Serenade." Historical Note for Royal Ballet Programme, 1964.

"Staging Balanchine Ballets: Una Kai Explains how she Reproduces his Works." *The Dancing Times,* No. 644 (May 1964), 418–419.

"A Wedding Bouquet." Historical Note for Royal Ballet Programme, 1964.

1965   "Le Baiser de la Fée." Historical Note for Royal Ballet Programme, 1965.

"Cinderella." Historical Note for Royal Ballet Programme, 1965.

A Gallery of Romantic Ballet. A Catalogue of the Collection of Dance Prints at the Mercury Theatre. With a Foreword by Dame Marie Rambert. London: New Mercury Ltd., 1965.

"Miss Forster—the First Bathilde." *The Dancing Times,* No. 661 (Oct. 1965), 22–23.

"A New History." [Review of] *A Concise History of Ballet* by Ferdinando Reyna. *The Dancing Times,* No. 661 (Oct. 1965), 29–31.

"Polovtsian Dances from Prince Igor." Historical Note for Royal Ballet Programme, 1965.

"Raymonda's History." *The Dancing Times,* No. 663 (Dec. 1965), 121–122.

"Romeo and Juliet." Historical Note for Royal Ballet Programme, 1965.

1966   "Apollo." Historical Note for Royal Ballet Programme, 1966.

A Bibliography of the Dance Collection of Doris Niles and Serge Leslie. [Review of.] *Theatre Research/Recherches Théâtrales,* 8, No. 2 (1966), 110.

"Card Game." Historical Note for Royal Ballet Programme, 1966.

"A Fanny Elssler Portrait." *The Dancing Times,* No. 668 (May 1966), 410–411.

"The History of Beatrix." Programme Note for Jack Carter's ballet *Beatrix (La Jolie Fille de Gand).* Festival Ballet, Aug. 1966.

"La Jolie Fille de Gand." *The Dancing Times,* No. 671 (Aug. 1966), 573–575.

"Monotones." Historical Note for Royal Ballet Programme, 1966.

"Les Noces." Historical Note for Royal Ballet Programme, 1966.

"The Post-War Contribution to the History of British Ballet." *Theatre Notebook,* 21, No. 1 (Autumn 1966), 42–46.

The Romantic Ballet in Paris. With a Foreword by Dame Ninette de Valois. English ed. London: Pitman, 1966. [A Polish translation by Agnieszka Kreczmer was published by the Państwowy Instytut Wydawniczy, Warsaw, in 1978.]

The Romantic Ballet in Paris. With a Foreword by Lillian Moore. American ed. Middletown, Connecticut: Wesleyan University Press, 1966.

1967   "Antony Tudor." Biographical Note for Royal Ballet Programme, 1967.

"Ballet." *Oxford Companion to the Theatre,* 3rd ed., ed. by Phyllis Hartnoll. London: Oxford University Press, 68–77.

"The Cachucha Reborn." *The Dancing Times,* No. 685 (Oct. 1967), 18–21.

"Casse Noisette." *About the House,* 2, No. 8 (Christmas 1967), 4–11.

Copinger and Skone James on Copyright. 10th ed. by F.E. Skone James and E.P. Skone James. [Review of.] *Theatre Notebook,* 22, No. 2 (Winter 1967–68), 95.

"Coppélia." Historical Note for Royal Ballet Programme, 1967.

The Dancer's Heritage. A Short History of Ballet. 3rd ed. London: Dancing Times, 1967.

"Miss Lillian Moore, Dance historian." [Obituary for.] *The Times.* 4 Aug. 1967.

"Ondine at Covent Garden." *The Dancing Times,* No. 676 (Jan. 1967), 184.

"Roland Petit." Biographical Note for Royal Ballet Programme, 1967.

1968   *Ballet in England: A Bibliography and Survey* by F.S. Forrester. [Foreword by Ivor Guest.] London: The Library Association, 1968.

"Carlotta Zambelli." [Obituary for.] *The Dancing Times,* No. 691 (April 1968), 357–358.

"The Nutcracker." Historical Note for Royal Ballet Programme, 1968.

"The Pas de Quatre." Special publication of the British Ballet Organization, Feb. 1968.

"The Two Giselles of the Romantic Ballet." *The Dancing Times,* No. 699 (Dec. 1968), 139–141.

1969   "Another Sleeping Beauty." *About the House,* 3, No. 4 (Christmas 1969), 34–38.

Carlotta Zambelli. Revue de la Société de l'Histoire du Théâtre, 1969, 199–255.

Dandies and Dancers. Dance Perspectives, 37 (1969).

"Raymonda." Historical Note for Royal Ballet Programme, 1969.

1970   "Arthur Saint-Léon." *Dance Gazette,* Autumn 1970, 3–5.

"Carlotta Zambelli in Russia." *The Dancing Times,* No. 721 (Oct. 1970), 23–25, 34.

The Dancer's Heritage. A Short History of Ballet. 4th ed. London: Dancing Times, 1970.

"Facade." Historical Note for Royal Ballet Programme, 1970.

Fanny Elssler. The Pagan Ballerina. London: A. & C. Black, and Middletown, Connecticut: Wesleyan University Press, 1970.

Giselle. [Jacket Notes on "The Creation of Giselle" and "Carlotta Grisi."] Cond. Richard Bonynge, Orchestre

National de l'Opéra de Monte-Carlo. Decca SET433–34, 1970.

"Job." Historical Note for Royal Ballet Programme, 1970.

"A Name to Cherish." [Part of "Adeline Genée—In Memoriam."] *Dance Gazette,* Summer 1970, 5–6.

The Pas de Quatre. London: London Dance Theatre Trust, 1970. [The facsimile score by Cesare Pugni with an Historical Introduction by Ivor Guest. A Japanese translation was published in 1976.]

Two Coppélias. A Centenary Study. London: Friends of Covent Garden, 1970.

1971   "Le Beau Danube." Programme Note for Festival Ballet, May 1971.

Coppélia. [Jacket Notes on "The Creation of Coppélia."] Cond. Ernest Ansermet, L'Orchestre de la Suisse Romande. Decca SET473–4, 1971.

"Ninette de Valois." Biographical Note for Royal Ballet Programme, 1971.

"Petrouchka." Programme Note for Festival Ballet, April 1971.

"Some Thoughts on Bournonville." *Dance Gazette,* 1971 (No. 2), 3–5.

1972   "Gautier's Centenary." *The Dancing Times,* No. 745 (Oct. 1972), 22–23.

The Romantic Ballet in England. 2nd ed., with a new Introduction. London: Pitman, and Middletown, Connecticut: Wesleyan University Press, 1972.

"La Sylphide—reconstructed." *Dance Gazette,* 1972 (No. 3), 3–4.

"Thackeray and the Ballet." *The Dancing Times,* No. 736 (Jan. 1972), 188–190.

"Victorian Friendship." [Review of] *Queen Victoria and the Bonapartes* by Theo Aronson. *Books and Bookmen,* 17, No. 11 (Aug. 1972), 44–45.

1973   "Fanny Elssler as the Swiss Milkmaid." *Harvard Library Bulletin,* 21, No. 1 (Jan. 1973), 73–74.

"Madame Dominique." *Dance Gazette,* 1973 (No. 2), 3–5.

"Michel Fokine." *Dictionary of American Biography.* Supplement Three, 1941–1945 (1973).

"Ursula Moreton 1903-1973." *Dance Gazette,* 1973 (No. 3), 3.

1974   *The Ballet of the Second Empire.* 2nd ed., comprising Vol. I
         1847-58 (1955) and Vol. II 1858-70 (1953), both works
         with a few corrections and a new Preface (replacing Serge
         Lifar's in Vol. II of the 1st ed). London: Pitman, and
         Middletown, Connecticut: Wesleyan University Press,
         1974.
         "La Bayadère." Programme Note for Théâtre National de
         l'Opéra, Spectacle de Ballets, Oct. 1974.
         "Carlotta Zambelli." *Dance Magazine,* 48. Part I—No. 2 (Feb.
         1974), 51-66; Part II—No. 3 (Mar. 1974), 43-58.
         Fanny Cerrito. The Story of a Romantic Ballerina. 2nd ed. Lon-
         don: Dance Books, 1974.
         "Manon in Nineteenth-century Ballet." *About the House,* 4,
         No. 5 (Spring 1974), 25-27.
         Nutcracker. [Jacket Notes.] Cond. Richard Bonynge, National
         Philharmonic Orchestra. Decca SXL6688-9, 1974.
         Sylvia. [Jacket Notes.] Cond. Richard Bonynge, New Philhar-
         monia Orchestra. Decca SXL6635-6, 1974.
         "The Year of the Great War." *Bush Telegraph,* Summer 1974,
         9. [Special publication to mark the Diamond Jubilee of
         the Bush Davies Schools.]

1975   "Ballet's Early Stages." [Review of] *The Pre-Romantic Ballet* by
         Marian Hannah Winter. *Books and Bookmen,* 20, No. 6
         (Mar. 1975), 38-39.
         Marco Spada. [Jacket Notes.] Cond. Richard Bonynge, London
         Symphony Orchestra. Decca SXL6707, 1975.
         Verdi Ballet Music. [Jacket Notes.] Cond. P. Maazel, Cleveland
         Orchestra. Decca SXL6726, 1975.

1976   *Le Ballet de l'Opéra de Paris. Trois siècles d'histoire et de tra-
         dition.* Trans. into French by Paul Alexandre. Paris: Paris
         Opéra, 1976. [A Japanese translation was published in
         1978.]
         "The Centenary of 'Sylvia.' " *Dance Gazette,* 1976 (No. 2),
         6-7.
         "Cyril Beaumont." [Obituary for.] *Dance Gazette,* 1976
         (No. 3), 16.
         Echoes of American Ballet. A Collection of Seventeen Articles

Written and Selected by Lillian Moore. Edited, and with an Introduction by Ivor Guest ["The Legacy of Lillian Moore."] New York: Dance Horizons, 1976.

"Le Pas de Six de La Vivandière." Programme Note for Le Ballet de l'Opéra, Soirée Romantique, 15 Sept. 1976.

"Le Pas Livry." Programme Note for *La Sylphide,* Théâtre National de l'Opéra, [23 Dec. 1976].

1977   "Carlotta Zambelli." *The Encyclopedia of Dance and Ballet,* ed. by Mary Clarke and David Vaughan. London: Pitman, 1977.

The Dancer's Heritage. A Short History of Ballet. 5th ed. London: Dancing Times, 1977.

The Divine Virginia. A Biography of Virginia Zucchi. New York and Basel: Marcel Dekker, 1977.

"Fanny Cerrito." *The Encyclopedia of Dance and Ballet,* ed. by Mary Clarke and David Vaughan. London: Pitman, 1977.

"Fanny Elssler." *The Encyclopedia of Dance and Ballet,* ed. by Mary Clarke and David Vaughan. London: Pitman, 1977.

"*La Fille mal gardée:* New Light on the Original Production." *Dance Chronicle,* 1, No. 1 (1977), 3–7.

Lettres d'un Maître de ballet. Correspondance d'Arthur Saint-Léon, accompagnée de notes et références et précédée d'une introduction par Ivor Guest. Trans. Odile de Lalain. *Revue de la Société d'Histoire du Théâtre,* 1977 (No. 3), 205–312.

"Paris Opéra Ballet." *The Encyclopedia of Dance and Ballet,* ed. by Mary Clarke and David Vaughan. London: Pitman, 1977.

"Paulette Dynalix." *The Encyclopedia of Dance and Ballet,* ed. by Mary Clarke and David Vaughan. London: Pitman, 1977.

The Pre-Romantic Ballet by Marian Hannah Winter. [Review of.] *Theatre Notebook,* 31, No. 2 (1977), 40–42.

"The Romantic Ballet." *Theatre Museum Card 10.* London: H.M.S.O., 1977.

Swan Lake. [Jacket Notes.] Cond. Richard Bonynge, National Philharmonic Orchestra. Decca D37D3, 1977.

"Virginia Zucchi." *The Encyclopedia of Dance and Ballet,* ed.

by Mary Clarke and David Vaughan. London: Pitman, 1977.

"Virginia Zucchi, The 'Divine' Inspiration of Russian Ballet." *The Dancing Times,* No. 797 (Feb. 1977), 263–264.

1978 "Adeline Genée." *Theatre Museum Card 44.* London: H.M.S.O., 1978.

"Adeline Genée 1878–1970." *Dance Gazette,* 1978 (No. 1), 9–12.

Adeline Genée. A Pictorial Record. With a Foreword by Dame Margot Fonteyn. London: The Royal Academy of Dancing, 1978.

"C. Wilhelm." *Theatre Museum Card 35.* London: H.M.S.O., 1978.

"Pas de Six from La Vivandière." Programme Note for the Joffrey Ballet, 1978.

"The Royal Academy of Dancing." *Theatre Museum Card 45.* London: H.M.S.O., 1978.

"To Genée with Love: The Sketches of Claire Avery." *The Dancing Times,* No. 811 (Apr. 1978), 404–405.

1979 "Les Biches." Historical Note for Royal Ballet Programme, 1979.

"Bournonville—at last!" [Review of *My Theatre Life* by August Bournonville, translated from the Danish and annotated by Patricia N. McAndrew.] *The Dancing Times,* No. 828 (Sept. 1979), 781.

"Cesare Pugni." *Dance Gazette,* 1979 (No. 1), 22–24.

"Finding Out about Fanny." *The Dancing Times,* No. 821 (Feb. 1979), 284–286.

"Margot Fonteyn, A Tribute." *Dance Gazette,* 1979, (No. 2), 9–10.

"The Romantic Ballet in Paris 1820–1850," in *Paris: The Romantic Epoch.* Washington, D.C.: John F. Kennedy Center for the Performing Arts, 1979, 52–59.

1980 "Donizetti's Ballet Music." [Jacket Notes.] Cond. Antonio de Almeida, Philharmonia Orchestra. Phillips 9500 673.

"Emma Livry." Note to accompany color illustration of Barre's statuette. *Dance Gazette,* 1980 (No. 2), 52–53.

"L'Era Romantica." Programme Notes on the Défilé, *Variations for Four, Nathalie, Esmeralda, La Péri, Robert le*

Diable and *Pas de Quatre* for the 8th International Cervantes Festival, Guanajato, Mexico, May 1980.

Gordon Craig on Movement and Dance, edited by Arnold Rood. [Review of.] *Theatre Research International,* V, No. 3 (1980), 246–247.

"Papillon." Programme Note for Sadler's Wells Royal Ballet, Feb. 1980.

"Paquita." Programme Note for Sadler's Wells Royal Ballet, May 1980.

"A Pilgrimage to Copenhagen. The Bournonville Festival." Written in collaboration with Ann Guest. *Dance Gazette,* 1980 (No. 1), 24–26.

The Romantic Ballet in Paris. 2nd ed., incorporating a few corrections and including Prefaces by Dame Ninette de Valois and Lillian Moore. London: Dance Books, 1980.

Victorian Ballet Girl. 2nd ed., incorporating a few corrections. New York: Da Capo, 1980.

1981   "Le Ballet de la paille." *Ballet/Danse,* No. 5 (Feb.–April 1981), 120–122.

"Costume and the Nineteenth Century Dancer." In *Designing for the Dancer.* London: Elron Press, 1981. 33–64.

"Fanny Elssler's Cachucha—Its Significance and its Preservation." In *Fanny Elssler's Cachucha,* by Ann Hutchinson. London: Dance Books, and New York: Theatre Arts Books, 1981. 11–16.

"Friedrich Albert Zorn. A Biographical Note." In *Fanny Elssler's Cachucha,* by Ann Hutchinson. London: Dance Books, and New York: Theatre Arts Books, 1981. 58–59.

Letters from a Ballet-Master. The Correspondence of Arthur Saint-Léon. Ed. Ivor Guest, with a few corrections to the French edition (1977). London: Dance Books, and New York: Dance Horizons, 1981.

"La Naissance de Coppélia." *Ballet/Danse,* No. 4 (Nov. 1980–Jan. 1981), 47–50.

Spotlight. [Catalogue of an exhibition of] *Four Centuries of Ballet Costume.* London: Victoria & Albert Museum, 8 April to 26 July 1981. Entries for Section 2 (18th and 19th Centuries) by Ivor Guest, 17–36.

Index

www.ingramcontent.com/pod-product-compliance
Lightning Source LLC
Chambersburg PA
CBHW021828090426
42811CB00032B/2070/J